THE CENTER SCRIPTURES

the Core Christian Experience

THE
CENTER SCRIPTURES

the Core Christian Experience

ROBLEY EDWARD WHITSON

THE UNITED INSTITUTE

Published by
The United Institute

Distributed by
Wyndham Hall Press   *Post Office Box 877, Bristol, IN 46507*

ISBN: 1-55605-009-7

Library of Congress Catalog Number: 87-050797

Contents

INTRODUCTION

You search the Scriptures
Because you think that in them
you have Eternal Life!
But they themselves bear witness to *me*,
and yet you refuse to come to *me*
to have Life!   (Jn. 5:39)

1   At the center of Christianity is Jesus Christ: Jesus of Nazareth, an historic human being "like us in everything" who is united within the Eternal Christ, "God Anointing", and so actually embodies All–God–is. He is the personal Union of the human and the Divine. The core of the Christian experience is the recognition of the living Christ and the recognition within him of the Fullness of God—*to know me is to know the Father.* There are many ways to speak of this and all it implies. Some of these ways come down to us in the words of the earliest communities, words later gathered together to form the Christian Scriptures. These Scriptures in themselves are not *the truth* nor do they transmit to us *divine truths for the*

1

mind—the Scriptures are witnesses to the Reality of Christ, that unique Person *who himself IS the Eternal Truth.*

The earliest of the Christian Scriptures are letters, beginning with the circular letter of James (c.45 AD) and the first letters of Paul. The process of collecting the Apostolic writings, ultimately forming the New Testament corpus, is initiated in the Pauline communities as they gather their teacher's letters. In preparing this earliest collection they apparently compose an introduction and summary of his teachings and give them the forms of letters—Ephesians and Colossians. As a literary form, *letters* suppose a specific context for our experience: we are listening to *someone speaking with us*, and it is a listening which expects a *response.* Letters are expressions of community, persons–with–persons, and all the participants are actively engaged in *speaking–listening–responding.*

We must be alert to the intention of the earliest communities as they used the form of letters to give shape to their words of witness. Letters are not treatises, doctrinal formularies or the like. They are interpersonal dialogic expressions of ongoing experience that is shared. Unlike the expectation implied in a historic narrative or prophetic oracle or statement of revelation or any of the other forms the Sacred Writings of the various Traditions have taken, a *letter* does not allow for a passive reader. An Apostle *writes* to a community because he cannot be there in the flesh at the moment, but his words are *read out* and *he* is heard speaking. And, as when he is present personally, the members of the community speak up with their responses, which are varied in the many ways which reflect their many distinct experiences. Speaking–listening—responding is the basic pattern in the shared experience of the first communities. They have heard the Good News—Christ—proclaimed by the first witnesses, and have responded in the mystery of recognition: Faith. Thus the speaking–listening–responding of letters is the most natural mode for their expression of further witness. Even writings that never could have been actual letters were given the formal shape of letters—the Gospel of Luke (Lk. 1:1-4), the Acts of the Apostles (Acts 1:1) with their patronal dedication formulas; the Apocalypse (Apoc. 1:4; 2:1; 2:8; 2:12; 2:18; 3:1; 3:7; 3:14).

Letters are personal communications to other persons. These letters came to be regarded as Scriptures. They expressed the witness to Christ among the communities which became the spiritual parents to further generations. They became *our* letters, handed on by our parents so we too could listen–and–respond. We realize that in them we hear *inspired* witness—not in the words or ideas as such (as if disembodied), but in the *inspired speakers*, people who *move in the Spirit* and so are consciously alive in Christ as Christ is in them. We listen to these inspired witnesses as they speak and we too find ourselves *moving, alive through the Spirit, consciously within Christ*.

2   Those portions of the Scriptures which most directly speak to the Reality of Christ as we experience him–us alive together are gathered here as the *center* of the Scriptures. The Letters/Gospels speak of many things— memories, realizations, concerns, questions—all radiating out from the Center, Christ. Some passages speak in depth of the experience of that Center with a special power. Listening to these Center Scriptures first, we will then be able to hear and grasp the witness of the others radiating out in so many directions. The various texts often underwent a long and complex process to reach their present shape. This process and the final shape represent the developing consciousness of the initial communities, and this is what we hear as we listen. Analysis of the texts gives us insight into that process, but it is the final shape of the words which is the witness of the communities–of–Faith to us. Thus, we can easily detect the many once-separate statements which were drawn together to form the present Last Supper Discourse. But it is the completed Discourse which is the witness to the full scope of the Faith experience of the Johannine community.

Rather than reshape the texts into a literary style in keeping with our contemporary language, the texts have been translated to reflect more directly the original manner of expression, thereby seeking to preserve special emphases and overtones of meaning all too easily lost. The phrasings of the original are represented by patterning the texts into sense–lines, a device designed to arrest our attention at each element of experience. As far as possible the word orders of the originals have been preserved, as have some of the special words and Semiticisms which carry subtle nuances of meaning. For example, there is a group of words coined by the early Greek communities to express a high sense of integral unity, words compounded with the prefix *syn*–; these have been rendered "—together–with" (as *syndoxasthomen* "we are glorified–together–with him" Rm. 8:17, in order to preserve the all–important emphasis of our totally integral unity within Christ in his Divine Glory). Or as with the Semiticism "Amen! I say to you. . .", the phrase especially emphasizes the concreteness of the Faith-experience in the ancient rabbinic exclamation of "Amen!" as *aman*, the steadfastness of faith; attention is thus drawn to the Hebrew sense of faith not as an act of trust in "leaping into the dark" but as a direct and solid experience of Reality (as solid as the image of rock so often used as the sign of faith). In addition, a few special translation decisions were made for the sake of the original *intentionality* which might not be evident in the external structure of the text. Thus, for example, the images of the Spirit are consistently feminine in character (in keeping with the feminine gender of the original Hebrew *Ruah*) and therefore the references to the *implied* gender–image have been rendered "she/her" rather than "he/his".

Each section of text is accompanied by an exploration of meanings. This is not intended to be a scripture–commentary, nor is it a developing scriptural theology. The core experience is being *explored* through these central scriptural expressions. Of course technical commentary material has been absorbed into these explorations, as have theological implications. But the emphasis is upon the attempt to make explicit the innermost significance of the Christian experience:
Christ the Union—God–Man–men–women.

The explorations seek to avoid identification with any one school of theological thought, and hence the utilizing of common words as the "technical" terms, usually employing the device of capitalization to highlight their special use (thus: Union, Life, Love, the Given, the Giving, and so forth). Throughout the explorations there are repetitions of terms (such as the many instances of "experience") inevitable because of the concentration of attention on their significance for this core area and the attempt to maintain a sharp focus upon the experiential, personal, interpersonal and related categories. And between sections there are inevitable overlappings of themes and expositions. Since all the explorations are designed to form a multiple resource rather than a single and unified presentation, some repetition of material is perhaps unavoidable, even though in each instance there are differing emphases.

In various sections attention is drawn to scriptural terms with special meanings operative in the first century, meanings often quite different from the original ancient meanings or from what might seem to be the literal meaning. Thus—

> *Heaven, heavenly*: originally an element of archaic cosmology,
> the Heaven–place above the firmament imagined as the realm
> of God where He dwelt; later the common way to refer to God

and the Divine, especially as a device of reverence to avoid us-ing the word 'God' in common speech. And so 'the Father in Heaven' or 'the Heavenly Father' means simply 'the Divine Father', 'Father–God'; and 'to come down from Heaven' means simply 'to come from God'.

Eternal Life: again Eternity and Eternal are reverential ways of referring to God and the Divine; 'Eternal Life', thus, does not mean 'endless Life' but 'Divine Life'.

Spirit and Name: the common ways of referring to person-hood or selfhood (for which there were no available abstract or substantive terms).

As is evident, these and similar linguistic evolutions from the more an-cient Hebrew through Aramaic of the post–Exilic period into the first cen-tury Greek of the Apostolic communities are crucial to our understanding of the expression of the scriptural experience. Christ "come down from Heaven" meaning come forth from within God is vastly different from the image of him as leaving a Heaven–place and relocating upon the earth.

Throughout the texts and commentaries the word "Church" has been rendered "Gathering". The intention of the original greek word Ekklesia is to stress a community of persons who have been called together one-by–one and who now form a unified Gathering of persons. Unfortunate-ly, the word "Church" all too often suggests a place or organization—a "thing" rather than people. Restoring the meaning of Ekklesia as Gather-ing is crucial for a realistic recognition of both the original Christian ex-perience and our contemporary quest.

3   The Scriptures are not the Word of God. Christ alone is the Word. The Scriptures are words about the Word of God—words spoken by inspired people who lived in Christ through the Spirit, and so more and more recognized and realized him/themselves alive–within–God. At the beginning of the second century, as the eldest generation was passing away and leav-ing the ministry of witness to those they had raised up, we hear Ignatius of Antioch speaking to the community gathered at Philadelphia. The dif-ference between Christ the living Word of God and the witnessing words about him is clear—

When I heard some say:

If I do not find it in the original Scriptures
I do not believe it is in the Good News—
I answer:
Yes, but it *is* written there. . .
it is Jesus Christ *who is* the original Scriptures:
the inviolable writings are
his Cross and Death and his Resurrection
and the Faith coming through him.
It is by these
and through your prayer
that I would be rendered upright!

(Letter to the Philadelphians 8:12)

The Reality actually experienced is centered in the Person Jesus Christ, not words. And it is the Christ experienced as he now fully is—as we are unified within him. From within that integral unity we share, it is clear that the words we speak and hear are *ours* as we bear witness to our real experience. Christ alone is the true Word of God, who does not speak to us *about* God but is the One through whom we ourselves enter into the full Reality of God. This is the Faith experienced by Ignatius and all the other first witnesses; it is the unifying prayer of the whole community of Faith which is the Thanksgiving, the Eucharist—the living response to the Self–gift of God in Christ.

Persevere in Prayer,
watchful in it
with Thanksgiving—
also praying together for us
that God may open to us
a door of the Word
to speak the Mystery of Christ.   (Col. 4:2-3)

one

THE GOOD NEWS: CHRIST THE MYSTERY

THE GOOD NEWS IN CHRIST

1   The scene which is "The beginning of the Good News of Jesus Christ" (Mk.1:1) is the same in each of the four Gospel accounts: John the Baptist in his ministry recognizing Jesus as the one who was to come. The Gospel of John, with extraordinary simplicity, unfolds the meaning of that recognition in the original disciples. This is the seed of their experience which will grow into the full vision of Faith.

John 1

35   The next day John was standing with two of his disciples
36   and, seeing Jesus walking by, said:
Look! The Lamb of God!
37   And the two disciples heard what he said
and they followed after Jesus.
38   Turning around and seeing them following

Jesus said to them:
What are you seeking?
And they said to him:
Rabbi—which translated means Teacher—
where do you live?

39 He said to them:
Come and see.
So they went and saw where he lived,
and stayed with him that day.
. . .

41 Next morning Andrew met his brother Simon
and said to him:
We have found the Messiah—
which translated means The Anointed.

42 He led him to Jesus. . .

43 The next day he decided to go to Galilee
and he met Philip.
And Jesus said to him: Follow me!
. . .

45 Philip found Nathanael and said to him:
We have found the one about whom
Moses wrote in the Torah
and the prophets wrote,
Jesus son of Joseph from Nazareth.

Disciples are seekers, those who seek to learn. The first word they address to Christ, "Rabbi—Teacher", expresses their expectation: here is one who can lead us to know. But logically they should have asked: Teacher, what can you tell us, what are your teachings and interpretations? And he should have answered: Come and you will study, you will understand. But—

Where do you live?
Come and see.
They went and saw and stayed with him.

The beginning–point of the Christian experience is not ideas, but a *person*, Jesus Christ. The center of Faith is a person, not a thing. And so *to learn* from him we must *live* with him, sharing life experience person-with-person. For we are not seeking to learn some *thing* from him, but to *recognize* him in all that he is.

The irreducible center of the Christian experience is the person Christ and all the persons sharing Life with him unitively. All the other Traditions have some *thing* at their center. We discover this quickly when we ask those who live by them what the central meaning of their Tradition is.

The Jew will reply with the commitment of the Covenant: Observe the precepts of the Torah from your heart.

The Muslim will reply unhesitatingly with the declaration of faith: There is no God but God, and Mohammed is the Messenger of God.

The Hindu will reply with the call to realize the inherent Wholeness of the All-One, Brahman-Atman, "not this" and "not that".

The Buddhist will reply with the liberating formula of the Four Holy Truths fulfilled in the Noble Eight-Fold Path to Enlightenment.

The Taoist will reply with the paradoxes of Inner Vision.

The Confucianist will reply with the Way of Ritual as it manifests the Harmony of Earth and Heaven.

The Christian must reply: Jesus Christ—a person, not a thing or idea or doctrine. However holy and enlightening all other centers of experience are, this center is a human being.

2   The apparent illogic of "Rabbi, where do you live" and "Come and see" yields to the realization that this is indeed the right way to express our experience of the Good News. Because he himself *is* the Good News. He has not come as a messenger to tell us some *thing*, to deliver a prophetic *word of God*. He is the Message, He alone is the Word of God!

This Good News did not fulfill the actual expectations of Ancient Israel (although Christians from their new perspective of experience would be able to assimilate aspects of the prophetic traditions). John the Baptist and all raised with him had looked forward to a coming Day of the Lord when God would reveal Himself in a new and final way. God would teach the full meaning of the precepts of the Torah and inspire people from within to observe them from their hearts out of delight, not fear. A Kingdom of peace, justice and holiness would embrace all peoples, uniting them in a perfect human life. Jerusalem, centered on the Temple of His Presence, would be the center of the world's worship and praise, and from it would come the healing of the nations. There in the Holy City would dwell the Anointed One reigning in God's Name in an endless dynasty. Even when we allow for awareness of the symbolic quality of these images, the expectation is clear: the one who was to come would bring these gifts, *these things*.

But when he came those who were able to recognize him eventually realized *He is the Gift*, He is *God Given* to us, the Gift to be *truly ours*. He does not teach about life, he is Life itself. The final meaning of the precepts of the Torah is Love and this cannot really be *commanded* since for any love to be *love* it must be *free* in persons who respond from depth to one another unitively. The Gift is not a mere perfecting of human life but the opening into Divine Life, to begin to exist within God as God is. And so we must come to live in Union, truly One in Life with Christ, God Given in Love—and so he–and–we together are to be the Temple of His Presence, a dwelling of living stones universally present wherever we are.

All this is in seed in the experience which begins the ministry of Christ. The first disciples of John went and saw, staying with him that day. And then they went out to others with the Good News: We have found *him!*—first Andrew to his brother Simon Peter, next Jesus calls Philip and then Philip to Nathanael. When Philip tells Nathanael who it is they have found—Jesus from Nazareth—Nathanael objects: "Can anything good come from Nazareth?" but Philip answers, "Come and see!" (v.46). Nathanael's objection is about a *thing*; Philip answers with the challenge of the direct experience of a *person*. (Later, in John 7, a similar point is made when the leaders of the people turn from the possibility of experiencing Jesus as they say: "Search the Scriptures and see that no prophet is raised up out of Galilee", v.52; because of a *thing*, the "word of God", they refuse to see *the person*, the Word of God.)

3   As in this initial scene of Christ's ministry—"Come and see"—and the beginning ministries of Andrew to Simon Peter and Philip to Nathanael, we find that the communities of Paul have been formed in Faith by this same call to *experience person*. In Colossians they preserve Paul's realization of the ministry of the Good News rooted in his own experience of Christ as a calling...

Colossians 1

24   on behalf of his Body which is the Gathering,
25   of which I became a minister
       to bring the message of God to fulfillment
26   the Mystery hidden for ages and generations
       but now manifested to His saints
27   to whom God wished to make known among the peoples
       the Wealth of the Glory of this Mystery
       Who is Christ–in–you,
       the hope of Glory,
28   whom we proclaim
       alerting everyone and teaching everyone
       in all wisdom
       so that we may present everyone mature in Christ.
29   And for this I labor
       striving with his own energy
       which works within me in Power.

"The Wealth of the Glory of this Mystery Who is Christ–in–you" is a striking expression of this experience of person. The phrase involves three levels of image: the *Mystery* as the always hidden reality of God, the *Glory* of this Mystery as the hidden Godhead is manifested in our sense of God's awe–inspiring Presence, and the *Wealth* of the hidden yet overwhelming God as that which enriches. Obviously the Wealth–image points from God to us: the Glory of the Mystery hidden from the beginning but now opened to all the Holy Ones enriches *us*, not God. The Greek nouns *doxa* (glory) and *mysterion* (mystery) are feminine and neuter in gender respectively; *ploutos* (wealth) is masculine as is the pronoun, and thus the grammatical structure of the phrase underscores the person–impact. Christ is not Glory or Mystery—*things*—but *He Who enriches since He is the Divine Wealth.* Yet it is not a mysterious Eternal Christ nor a single individual Jesus the glorious Christ. It is the Wealth Who is Christ–in–you (and the Greek "you" here is the plural). The Eternal Christ is the All that God is. Embodied concretely in the human person Jesus, this All he receives from the Father is the Wealth given through him to everyone, enriching all. The Christ–in–us is the total interpersonal Union who are the Wealth previously hidden within God but now embodied as the All in all. Expectations about a mystery to be revealed logically lead us to look for a thing—truth, doctrine, idea—but in Christ-in-us we discover person.

It is the Mystery Who is Christ-in-you. It is not the single person Christ, but as he is "in you", the plural "you". The Good News that God has finally revealed His Mystery is not Good News about someone else— it is Good News about us. Paul's calling is "on behalf of his Body which is the Gathering. . .to bring the message to fulfillment". He serves the full Christ (the only one there is) as he actually lives now: in-through-with all who are drawn into Union with him. It is from within the Reality of Christ that we can recognize the Mystery being unveiled in him-us. This is the One Paul proclaims in the God News "alerting and teaching everyone in all wisdom". And, once again, this proclaiming of wisdom is not identified as a function of the mind, some "thing-wisdom" to be grasped.

4   I Corinthians 2

> 6 We speak the Wisdom of God
>   in Mystery
> 7 which has lain hidden
>   but which before the ages
>   God has destined for our Glory.
> 8 Not one of the leaders of this age has known it,
>   for if they had known
> 9 they would not have crucified
>   the Lord of Glory.
>   But as has been written:
>   *things the eye has not seen*
>   *and the ear has not heard,*
>   *which have not come into anyone's heart—*
>   *all these God has prepared*
>   *for those who love Him.*

The Wisdom of God is the Lord of Glory. He is the Mystery who cannot be *known about*: he must be recognized as a person by other persons. This is the Wisdom of God's Spirit and of humans' spirits—*spirit*: the inner, unique living-selfhood.

THE GOOD NEWS IN US

I Corinthians 2

10 For God has revealed all these to us
through the Spirit,
for the Spirit reaches into all things,
even the Depths of God.
11 For among men
who knows the depths of a man
except the spirit of a man within him?

1   The Spirit, the inner living–Selfhood of God, alone can plumb the
Depths of the hidden reality God is. The spirit of each individual alone
can plumb the depths of each unique person. It is a simple self–reflective
truth: only I myself can know from deep within myself what it is to be *me*.
Each person as person is unique, truly unlike any other, and therefore unable
to be compared with any other—no word or concept can realistically represent the unique person to the mind. Self can only be known by self.
    The Spirit of God is at the center–Depth of God, and at the center-
depth of us all, as we arise into personal existence from that One Source.
But our existence is transformed as that innermost Self becomes our Gift.

12 And we have not received
the spirit of the world
but the Spirit of God
so that we may know
the Depths freely given us by God.

2   We are to be fulfilled not by a natural inner selfhood (the spirit of the
world) but by the Divine Selfhood. By the Union of Self–with–self we are
at the Depths of God, and we begin to *know* as only person can know:
from within what it is to be Me.

13 And we speak not in words taught by human wisdom
but in words taught by the Spirit,

interpreting the spiritual by the spiritual.
14   But the only–logical man
      does not accept
      the Depths of the Spirit of God,
      for they are foolishness to him
      and he cannot perceive them
      because in their inner reality
      they must be assessed spiritually.
15   But the spiritual man
      assesses all things in their inner reality
      yet in his own inner reality
      he is assessed by no one.

3   The "words" taught by the Spirit are not words at all—in the sense of concepts, representations of the mind. These "words", rather, are the inner movements of person in which, mysteriously, one person is able *to touch* and *be touched by* another: that awakening to each other which is what we mean by *recognition* in its deepest sense. One who approaches others with intellect–only will know them as things, not persons. And intellect–only will know God only as an idea, not the inner Reality of Self–Giving.

16   *For who knows the mind of the Lord,*
      who will instruct Him?
      But we have the Mind of Christ!

4   II Corinthians 3

17   For the Lord is the Spirit
      and where the Spirit of the Lord is,
      there is freedom.
18   All of us with our faces unveiled
      as we reflect the Glory of the Lord
      are actually being transformed
      from Glory to Glory
      into that very reflection–image
      by the Lord, the Spirit.

The Good News is not about Jesus only, it includes all of us together.

It is the news of Jesus, *Yeshua*, "the Liberator", and so it is the news of Freedom—that Freedom which alone belongs to God. We yearn for and prize every experience of personal freedom, even as we feel bounded by the inevitable limits of our lives which are so clearly circumscribed by the relativity of our existence. We are not absolute beings: we depend, we need, we die. God does not. God absolutely is. God needs no one and no thing, and so alone is free.

The Good News is the Mystery: the unneeding God gives Himself to us—Given once–for–all in the Eternal Christ centered in Jesus the Anointed, and endlessly Giving in our Spirit lives as we are drawn into Union within him. As we grow in our recognition of him we grow in our self–transformation, becoming the very Image we see. This is the ongoing living out of the Christ Life, from Glory to Glory, the ever–deepening recognition of persons–together.

> Now we can only see a blur
> as in a mirror reflection,
> but then it will be face to face!
> Now I only know a fragment
> but then I shall fully know
> just as I am fully known!   (I Cor. 13:12)

5   As in the response of the very first disciples *when they found him*, this Gift of Christ Life remains absolutely free. It does not become the *possession* of the one who receives. In the transforming Spirit there is the Power to bring forth more Life, the urge from deep within *to give*. This becomes our Gospel Ministry, to bear living witness so that still others can awaken to the wonder we all become in Christ.

6   II Corinthians 4

> 4   The "god" of this age
> has blinded the thought
> of those who disbelieve
> so there will not shine forth
> the enlightenment of the Good News
> of the Glory of Christ
> who is the Image of God.

> 5 For we do not proclaim ourselves
>   but Christ Jesus the Lord
>   and ourselves your servants
>   for the sake of Jesus.
> 6 The God Who said:
>   *Let light shine out of darkness*
>   is He Who has shone in our hearts
>   to be the radiance of our consciousness
>   of the Glory of God
>   on the face of Christ.

In the creation symbol of Genesis, God creates light at the very center of the chaos of darkness—and the light blazes forth dispelling the dark. But in Christ we discover that God Himself *is* the Light blazing within us at our very center of personal existence. And so we seek no illumination from outside to know Christ, for our consciousness is illuminated from within. We recognize the face of Christ—the person—shining with the Glory of God because we radiate that same Glory as persons–together transformed in God's Self–Gift.

7   Galatians 4

> 4 When the fullness of time came
>   God sent forth His Son
>   born of a woman
>   born under the Law
> 5 so that he might free those under the Law
>   that we might receive the adoption of sons.
> 6 And because you are sons
>   God has sent forth the Spirit of His Son
>   into our hearts crying out: Abba!—Father!

God sent forth His Son—God is Given—so that we can become sons—truly *receive* this Self–Gift. Paul insists that this experience of transformation is not an approximation or analogy. The adoption of sons is not the experience of becoming *something like* the Only Son. It is truly becoming All he is. The transformation is to be complete: we are to be filled with the entire Fullness of God (Eph. 3:19). It is the symbol of adoption which is the metaphor. In human adoption the child is treated as if he were an actual son, though, of course, he is not; in this Divine "adoption" we are treated as sons because we truly have become actual sons. As the ancient Fathers insist over and over, the only difference between ourselves and Christ is that we humans *have become* all he *eternally is*. The difference is only in *how* we are what we are: Christ by Nature, we by Gift.

And there are not many sons/daughters, but all are the Union of the One Son. For it is the singular Spirit of His Son which is Given us. The Divine Spirit of Christ—the inner living-Selfhood of Christ—is now ours, at the center of our unique personal existence. This Selfhood of Christ has not displaced the individual's own selfhood (anymore than it displaced the human selfhood of Jesus): the two are One in Union, sharing identity. As we truly share the ultimate Identity of Christ so he–we cry out recogniz-ing God as *Our Father*, with a word of intimacy and warmth, *Abba!*

8   Romans 8

> 14   For as many as are guided by the Spirit of God,
>   these are sons of God.
> 15   For you did not receive the spirit of slavery
>   once again bringing fear,
>   but you received a spirit of adoption
>   by which we cry out: Abba!—Father!
> 16   The Spirit Herself bears witness
>   together with our own spirit
>   that we are children of God.
> 17   If sons then also heirs
>   both heirs of God and heirs–together–with Christ
>   since we suffer–together–with him
>   so that we also may be glorified–together–with him.

The Spirit of God is recognized in the constant Giving of the inner-most Self of God. The Giving is identified as the Helper—Paraclete—in a clearly feminine image. Throughout the Hebrew Scriptures the Spirit suggests a mothering by God, as in the opening of Genesis with the Spirit hovering as a great mother bird alighting on her nest of creation. The very word *Ruah*, "Breath", "Breathing", is feminine in gender. (The Greek *Pneuma* translates *Ruah* directly, but is neuter in gender and hence a linquistic confusion is accidentally introduced, compounded by the Latin translation of *Spiritus* with its masculine gender.)

The Spirit is spoken of here as guiding us (not as moving or directing us). The intended meaning of the verb is clear: we are guided (literally: guided as on a journey) by the Spirit as we travel in life—we determine the journey and destination, and the Spirit enables us to find our way guiding our steps, but not taking our steps for us. It is the act of a Helper, a Guide. It is the supportive experience we associate with the loving mother.

Guided by the Spirit we are sons. We have not received the spirit of slaves. It is not a consciousness of creaturehood which dominates our sense of self. If we were left nothing more than creatures our ultimate relationship would only be to God as Creator—our calling would be to nothing more than obedience. But we have received the spirit of adoption. In the archaic Hebrew tradition descent is traced through the mother not the father, and hence adoption also takes place through a mother. We remember the beautiful scene of Ruth's adoption by Naomi in which the new daughter takes identity with her new mother: where you go I will go, where you live I will live, your people shall be my people, and your God my God (Ruth 1:16). And at the birth of a child it is the mother who presents the newborn to the father who then acknowledges his offspring.

This is Paul's image. In our rebirth through the Spirit we cry out to our Father "Abba!" Through Her we recognize Him. And we ourselves together with our Mother the Spirit bear a united witness that we truly are the Divine Offspring: She presents us and we cry out in recognition "Abba!"—our first and ultimate cry of new Life.

All the Father is He has Given in the Son and is ceaselessly Giving through the Spirit. And we become that One All. Thus Paul insists

> We are heirs–together–with Christ,
> since we suffer–together–with him,
> and are glorified–together–with him.

These last are specially coined words, designed to express a total shared identity: we are heirs–together–with him (*synkleronomoi*), since we *sympaschomen* and are *syndoxasthomen*. We suffer–together–with Christ in the one act of Life-giving as he pours himself out for us and we receive and so become One—his Gift is effective! And so we are glorified–together–

with him since we truly have become One in his Gift, and thus share in All he is, a Divine as well as human Unity.

9   The Good News is the Wisdom Who is Christ–in–us. It is the wonder: God is truly now one of us—and the unfolding response to that wonder: we become truly One in Him. This is the single center of the Christian experience of Faith, and so it is the unique norm of authenticity in all we attempt to understand (belief), to live (commitment) and to see (prayer).

At the very end of the second letter to the Corinthians Paul resolves all their struggle towards a unitive Life in Christ in proposing this one infallible examination of experience:

> Test yourselves
> to see if you are in the Faith,
> prove yourselves:
> do you not yourselves perceive
> Jesus–Christ–is–in–you
> (unless you are counterfeits!)?   (II Cor. 13:5)

This is the Good News—come and see!

two _____

TRANSFORMATION
LIFE—DEATH—RESURRECTION

INTRODUCTION

1   The four Gospel communities open their witness to the Faith of Easter with the Passover Supper whose eating and drinking will be the sign of the living Christ, the Meal which will become the Feast of the Lord for all who arise within him. The Transformation of Christ Life—in him and in us—begins with this final Meal.

As a simple daily reality a meal is a powerful sign of human life. In birth we are set free to begin independent personal lives. But the tangible process of life remains rooted in sustaining bodily life, in drawing the stuff of life from the living world around us: transforming *it* into *me*. Our first eating is the intimate drawing of nourishment from another person. The blood–given life of the womb gives way to a personal giving–and–receiving: as the infant drinks from his mother they are face–to–face. In a few weeks the experience of being mothered—being fed, held, made secure, kept warm—has become the experience of being loved, and the baby smiles, for the first time recognizing *that face*: the person who loves and now is loved in response. And so we grow into a greater meaning for personal life in those times of eating when we are together with others.

A meal person–with–person suggests the sharing of life. We know life is more than the body which is its root. It is not individual life alone which calls us to eat together, but full human life: *persons together*—each truly a person and all growing into an ever deeper sense of the ultimate unity that transcends the potential isolation of independence. A simple meal can be the sign of *lives which mean love*.

2   The Passover Meal centers upon the experience of freedom. Living communities remember their beginnings. Slavery is destroyed as death strikes down masters but passes over the enslaved. The liberated pass through the barrier of the sea to Sinai and the gift of Covenant and Torah. The now free–born pass into the new life of promise to dwell with the Presence of the Lord–in–Power. The Meal is not merely a memory of events now past and felt only in their effects. It is a present recognition: we are this community, living still, begetting new life, sharing life and consecrating life in the Gift of God.

It is the moment of this ancient Meal in which Christ begins to reveal himself: he begins to die so all can live. The Twelve Witnesses at table with him receive a Gift they cannot understand—until they recognize him again *in the breaking of bread*. The Paschal Meal and the Easter Feast, together, embody the Mystery of Christ. He is the Gift poured into their human lives transforming them into the New Life he is: God–and–Man All–One.

The Gospel community of John draws together into this beginning–moment of the Meal all the meanings they discover in their Transformation at the Feast. Who he was and has become, who they are and are becoming, all suggest a new language of Faith. The words and symbols learned in the past must now express the new heavens and new earth. What has been a promise always for the future has become present reality. The deepest visions of the prophets, the most exalted songs of prayer and the clearest words in the Scriptures were now seen to be but the faintest of hints. Even the initial experience of the Apostle as he had followed Jesus, coming to know him in all he said and did, had been only a shadow.

3   The community of John speaks a new language expressing their new experience. They seek to express the present, living reality of Christ with

their new understanding of all they had known. They are uninterested in recounting merely past events. They are giving witness to the total Transformation which has taken place. They are uninterested in the *shapes* of what has happened. They are concerned with the inner *meanings* revealed through the shapes. The tangible words and actions of Jesus are reshaped to allow the meanings to come forth. The language of their Faith–experience can even suggest speaking of the Paschal Meal without the words and actions of the bread and wine (obviously their central experience at each week's Lord's Day worship in Christ) so that the totality of life they signify cannot be obscured. They weave the many strands of his life of ministry among them into one great statement of Faith. Remembered words from hundreds of days are gathered into the short hours of one last evening.

We must remember that as they reckoned time the new day began with the sunset of the day just concluding. The Last Supper and Eucharist, then, were taking place in their experience not on "Thursday" but in the opening night–portion of Friday. In the unfolding of one day, beginning with his self–giving through the signs of bread and wine and culminating in the sacrificial laying down of his life, the disciples are swept from life through death to the threshold of new Life. The meaning of this Day of the Lord is proclaimed in the words of this once–for–all Feast of Life. For on that night at table began the final day of the old world—when it was finished on the Cross all things had been made New.

TRANSFORMATION IN CHRIST

John 13

1   It was before the Feast of the Passover.
Realizing his hour had come
to pass from this world to the Father
and loving those who were his in the world,
Jesus loved them to the end completely.

1   The Mystery of Christ is the living Christ himself. It is not a symbol or idea or doctrine.

Every actual person is a living mystery: who can know the inmost reality of a person but the person himself? (I Cor. 2:11) The living mystery of person can be affirmed by *names* which proclaim the uniqueness of each, but that uniqueness ultimately calls upon us to recognize the hiddenness of every person. Not one of us can be reduced to ideas of the mind and simply be *represented*. What can be spoken of are those aspects of human life we have in common. The wonder of unique personhood remains beyond concepts.

But we can come to know each other as persons—not by *knowing about* another, but by *really knowing: by touching* each other as persons, *by living* with each other as persons, *by participating* in each other as persons. In the natural mystery of human life, truly *unique* persons can become truly *one*. In the unity of persons we can come to really know one another. We can know because we ourselves participate in a unitive life. We experience one another in the depth of being persons when we love.

Jesus Christ is not a symbol, idea or doctrine to these first friends to whom he has opened his inmost life. He loves them, they love him. They know the Mystery of Christ because they participate in his life, and so they recognize who he fully is: the One come forth into their lives from within the Hidden God. Because they know–by–loving him, they can recognize the Hidden God to be Father—his, become theirs. And they know–by–love he has come into their lives to be One with them forever. As he passes from the world returning into the Father he does not go alone: all are drawn into the Father in the unity of Christ.

2   He loves them to the *very end*—to the culmination of his life with them, to the death that opens into New Life. He loves them to the end *completely*—pouring out his life for them, giving them that Life which is Love: *God is Love*. In the two–fold implication of *end* the community of John has found an expression for their experience of the absoluteness of the Love of Christ given them: he never ceased loving them to the very last moment, and his loving came to perfection for them as that moment opens into the Fullness of God.

This experienced Mystery of Christ is the *meaning* of the Transformation of living–dying–rising which unfolds. Jesus in whom the Fullness of God has come into human life makes us One by loving/giving himself absolutely so that we enter once–for–all within his Love. The meaning is expressed through the words and actions of the Paschal Meal as these embody the many moments of our awakening to the reality of who he–we together are. We have already died and risen in him, we are alive in his

New Life, we are hidden with him in God; who we fully are is still to be unveiled. (Col. 3:1-4) Yet we know–by–love the *persons* who are *becoming*. And so through these words and actions we can reflect our inner experience—Faith—as we live the Transformation.

GOD SERVES: GIFT

John 13

12   When he had washed their feet
       and put on his clothes and reclined again at table
       he said to them:
       Do you realize what I have done to you?
13   you call me Teacher and Lord
       and rightly, for I AM!
14   Therefore if I the Lord and Teacher
       washed your feet
       you should wash one another's feet.
15   I have given you an example:
       As I have done to you,
       you also should do.
16   Amen! Amen! I say to you:
       A servant is not greater than his master
       nor the messenger greater than the sender.
17   Now that you realize this
       if you do it you will be happy.
             . . .
20   Amen! Amen! I say to you:
       whoever receives the one I send
       receives me,
       and whoever receives me
       receives the One Who sent me.

1   The ancient ritual of washing as a purification for participation in a sacred meal is transformed at this Paschal Meal. A ceremonious act is radically reshaped into the clearest sign of the most personal service.

       It is so clear that Peter (representing us all) recoils. Washing feet is the menial task of slaves, or, in the rarest of instances, an extraordinary way in which a disciple might show deep reverence for a beloved and venerable teacher. The Teacher does not serve the disciple, nor the Lord those who should serve Him!

> *"You shall never wash my feet!"*
> *"If I do not wash you, you can have no share with me."*

This is no ritual to prepare for participation in a meal. It is the beginning of participation in Christ. In this sign Christ reveals what sharing with him means. And all the meaning must be accepted if we are to be One with him.

> *Do you realize what I have done to you?*

If we are to recognize and participate in Christ we must grasp this sign of Christ. All his further words and acts in the next hours have their first expression here. To understand all that is said as the Paschal Meal unfolds we must understand what he has just done.

We *think* we understand. It is the act of supreme humility. We think of it as a magnificent human act: the man Jesus acts as servant to others to show how humble our service to one another should be—he is the teacher showing loving reverence to his disciples so that when they in turn become the teachers they will love and revere those they seek to enlighten. Generation after generation of Christians have practiced footwashing as the sign of humble dedication, a sign which can have great beauty and power in its simplicity.

But all this is only the barest hint of the full meaning of the sign. We err in thinking of Jesus–the–man as showing us human humility.

> *Do you realize what I have done to you?*
> *You call me Teacher and Lord*
> *and rightly, for I AM!*

Christ cannot be divided into Jesus–the–man and, separately, God. He is one completely single individual who is unitively God–Man: truly human and fully Divine, as One. He can never be encountered except as he is *completely*. We may be *aware* of him only partially (as, indeed, were the first disciples until Easter) but that is our limitation, the partial character of our thought and words. Within the limits of our minds we have a fragmented vision of Christ, but Christ is always Whole: the one in whom the Fullness of God lives bodily. (Col. 2:9)

In his sign of serving, Christ proclaims that he is acting as Teacher and Lord. The two–fold affirmation is further emphasized by its reverse repetition. . . *if I the Lord and Teacher*. It is the Incarnate God—the Fullness alive in human life—Who serves. It is *the Lord* Who is Teacher. The Gospel community of John often affirms their realization of the Fullness–Who– is–Christ by recognizing in his own words the awesome Name of God, I AM. These are the words given to Moses when he insisted on knowing God's Name: *ehyeh asher ehyeh*, I AM WHAT I AM, tell them I AM sent you (Ex. 3:14). The name does not make God known. It insists on the ab solute Mystery of God: He cannot really be known by words or images, all of which must prove false. He is the Hidden God Whose Presence can be felt in His Power. Christ reveals the Hidden God Whose Presence can now be shared in His human life. As had been promised, when the fullness of time came, God Himself would be our Teacher. Christ acknowledges: indeed, Teacher and Lord I AM!

2   The Lord teaches us: *God serves us, we do not serve God!* And our first instinct is to draw back as Peter did. It is so unreasonable at first sight. It is the creature who serves, not the Creator. That is our natural insight in to our relationship to God, and it is one constantly proclaimed throughout the Torah and the Prophets. We depend absolutely on God, the One Source of existence, the One Will determining all good. He is One, there is no other, and He alone is to be adored. To obey and to serve are the responses of Faith. But as God fully reveals Himself in Christ He reveals: *I serve!*

We realize that God in no way needs anything from us. God alone sim ply *is*—Infinite, One, Absolute. Our attempts to serve God actually give Him *nothing*, and we know it. We have thought of our service, rather, as the concrete manifestation of our obedience, an obedience in loving response to the Will for our greatest good. We serve, to carry out that Will. But Christ came to do the Will of the Father: to give us the Living God.

To obey is not the willingness *to do something*, it is the willingness *to receive God in His giving*. We must be willing to be served *by God*. He alone can give us His Living Self and so we must be humble and receive. Taking is always a humbling experience for in it we implicitly acknowledge: *we need*. We imagine ourselves as secure or dominant or glorious as we take and possess things or even persons. Deep within we know the truth—*we need everything!* God alone can give All. Christ has come to serve, not to be served.

3   The meaning of service is radically transformed in this sign. We cannot share in Christ unless we are willing to receive What he gives. The Self–Gift of God is given to us freely, not forced upon us. He has given, unconditionally, whether or not we will receive, and He will never withdraw His Gift/Love. But if it is to be truly ours—our own in our freedom—we must make it ours. Christ's Gift of God to us is really a *gift*, not a disguise for control, manipulation or domination. Most of our experience of gifts is, sadly, not of gift at all. If something is "given" conditionally ("if you do this, then I will give. . ." or "you may keep this if. . .") then it is not *gift* but *price*. The experience is not giving–and–receiving, but negotiation. Small children are innocent enough to take gifts as gifts—with joy and in freedom. They do not yet realize that most often people give "gifts" with "strings attached"—and the receiver is thus not truly free in taking, but is entangled (benevolently or otherwise) in someone's *plan for him*. A true gift cannot be conditioned, cannot be taken back. For once it is freely given and received *it is mine!* God–in–Christ is truly Gift for us and that is why it can only come by *Christ serving.* In the Mystery of the Feast of the Lord we discover *God serves God to us,* and so we truly eat and drink Life.

God–in–Christ does not serve us for any *purpose.* It is not a means to an end. It is pure Gift: He loves, He is Love itself. In Christ we discover *God is Self–giving.* And as we reach out and receive so that this given Life is now actually our own, we ourselves can begin *to give God.*

as I have done to you, you also should do.

The servant messenger who proclaims the Good News does so not with words but with the Life lived. Receiving the messenger is the receiving of the service of Christ—the servant who has been served now serves others, the work of service giving–and–receiving, building up the living bodily Presence of God, given, incarnate, integrally One in human life.

Jesus loved them to the end, completely.

PRESENCE IN POWER

John 13

31   The Son of Man has already been glorified
      and God has been glorified in him.
      God will glorify him in Himself
      and will glorify him now

1   Glory belongs to God alone. All that comes into existence from God
reflects that Glory.

The word *glory* expresses our experience of awe when we are swept up
into a moment which overwhelms us with its power. Glory is not an experience of quiet. It bursts upon us.

We can experience glory in immense things or in the smallest, in things
of the greatest majesty or in the simplest—wherever we find ourselves over-
powered. Our experience of glory always occurs because the power encountered is inherent in the thing or person. It is not an external cir-
cumstance. The greater the power source, the greater the sense of awe, and
so the greater the affirmation of glory. As we recognize the ultimate Source
in God alone, He alone is glorious in Himself.

However much it attracts, the encounter with God is also awesome,
to the point of terror. From the beginning we have realized He *is* the Power
of Existence—in the most primitive human experience *life-and-death*: the
wonder of being brought to life, the terror of dying. Drawing near to this
Presence in Power, but not daring to reach out and "touch" or to look "face
to face", is the ancient celebration of Glory.

Such power was not to be found in creatures. Whatever our power, it
is but a dim reflection. When as humans we desire to proclaim "our own"
glory we must disguise ourselves with crowns, gold, dazzling jewels and rich
clothing, constrain ourselves to walk majestically and act toward others
so as to inspire the petty awe of envy or fear. Tragically, our great celebra-
tions of glory as human power are war, conquest and killing, to prove that
the power of life–and–death is ours. The lust for "glory" whether on a great
or small scale requires that we keep the truth from ourselves. But our powers
have their Source in Another, and deep within we know it. In pride we
hide this truth under glorious ornaments. Or in the freedom of simplicity
we rejoice in the truth that our glory is real indeed: our living power is

the loving Gift of His Glory.

2   If we are willing to live in the truth we quickly learn the paradox that what seem to be the powerless are actually the powerful, and so the real reflection of Glory.

> God chose the common and despised things of the world,
> those that are 'nothing',
> so that He might bring to nothing
> what seem to be everything. . .
> that as has been written:
> *Let anyone who boasts*
> *boast in the Lord.*   (I Cor. 2:23, 31)

At the center of the human tragedy of evil is the fact that we can regard other human beings as common and despised, as *nothings*. How often we find great value placed on *things* and none on *people*. When we look closely we see why: things can be possessed and their power (whatever it might be) taken to make the possessor seem more powerful, to enhance the illusion of glory. Persons *as persons* simply cannot be possessed. They can be constrained, harnessed and made to work, they can be deluded or terrorized to acclaim false glory, they can be dominated and used. But a truly human response must be *personal*: it must bear the character of the uniqueness of individuality and hence it must be freely given—from one unpossessable and no–other–like–it person to another. Among the creatures of our world it is living human persons who in their consciousness most powerfully reflect Glory. Contempt for others is the sign of how great a lie must be lived to avoid the truth of Glory. For those whose tragedy is more subtle, who acclaim all Glory to be God's while still trying to cling to the sense of power as their own this lie must be even greater—

> If anyone says:
> I love God—and hates his brother,
> he is a liar!
> For he who does not love his brother
> whom he has seen
> cannot love God
> Whom he has not seen.   (I Jn. 4:20)

How many have perished—died in so many ways—as others chanted *"For the greater Glory of God!"*

3   Christ *Son of Man* identifies himself in his glory with all of us. He reflects the Glory, the living Reality of God, as we can. He lives in the truth and loves all those who have come into his life—*he loves them to the end, completely.* As an actual human being he shows us what it would be like for us to live in love, to recognize in one another the clearest reflection of Glory, to take delight in the gift we can be for each other. Jesus has already been glorified and God has been glorified in him because he has lived his life in the awesome power that human love can be, and the disciples have witnessed it by participating in it. If they have learned nothing else with him they have learned what it is like to be loved completely.

Christ *Son of God* reveals his Glory to be the Glory of God Himself. He lives the Life of that Love Who is God. In the Transformation of life–into–Life experienced by all who become One in Christ we come to recognize he does not merely *possess* power for life, he *is* the Power of Life.

> And the Word became flesh
> and raised His Sanctuary–Tent among us
> and we saw his Glory:
> the Glory of the Only–Begotten of the Father
> full of Gift and Truth.   (Jn. 1:14)

God glorifies Christ in Himself, and glorifies him now. We know it because now we have been begotten into this Life and so have that Glory within us.

> Everyone who believes Jesus is the Anointed
> has been begotten of God,
> and everyone who loves Him Who begot
> loves him who has been begotten of Him.   (I Jn. 1:14)

COMMANDMENT: LOVE

John 13

34   I give you a new commandment,
      that you love one another—
      as I have loved you
35   By this will all know you are my disciples:
      if you have Love for one another.

1   The most rudimentary human life is built upon the reality of love, the *giving* of life. In the long months before birth, after that first "giving" of one cell to another in union, all the stuff of life is given, drawn from the bodily life of the mother. Our independent life at birth depends absolutely on the giving of another, not merely the stuff of life, but the warmth, assurance, affection and personal presence through which we can grow to be persons with other persons. From the very experience of our formation in life we know what it means to love and be loved—both when we have love and when love is denied.

The ancient command to love is not the imposition of a noble work upon us. It is the call to respond to how we must live to be who we can become, as we grow in the process of life–giving. When the people ask Jesus how to interpret the precepts of the Torah he draws together two commandments as the norm of life in the Way taught by the Law and the prophets. All the other (more than six hundred) commandments derive their meaning from the two–fold command to love:

Hear, O Israel, the Lord your God, the Lord is One!
And you shall love the Lord your God
with all your heart and with all your soul
and with all your mind and with all your strength.
You shall love your neighbor as yourself. (Deut. 6:15; Lev. 19:18)

There is no greater commandment than these. (Mk. 12:29-31)

2   As we need to be loved so we are to love others since they need love. This simple experience at the foundation of our lives is to be our response to the loving God Who gives us our living existence.

But in Christ we receive a new commandment of love, centered in the Transformation experienced in Christ. We are to love *just as he loves*. This is both human and Divine. He loves completely and he loves in that complete Self–giving Who is God. If we love *as he loves* we can be recognized to be his disciples, but only if it is *as he loves*. Human love of itself does not proclaim the Christ Presence; natural love is the urge at the core of our lives right from the beginning, and it is the command of uprightness in the Torah. The newness of his commandment is not to be found in its degree (that we love completely). Any reflection on our power to love tells us that, left to ourselves, we can never expect to love *completely*: there must always be limit, not necessarily from any unwillingness to love but simply from the fact of individual limitation. None of us in any way is infinite.

Jesus tells his disciples to love as he loves and in this they will find their identity. As it unfolds in the next few moments of their Meal together, he is about to promise them/us the Divine Power of Love, the Love in which he himself is loved by the Father. And in the space of a few hours they are to discover how truly complete his Love is as he gives us the Fullness of the Godhead to be our Life. To live as human beings in *that Love for all* who are alive with us will alone mark the transforming Christ dwelling within human life.

INNER DWELLING

John 14

2   In my Father's House there are many rooms. . .
    I am going now to prepare a place for you.
3   If I go and prepare a place for you
    I shall return again and take you with me
    so that where I am
    you also shall be.
4   And where I go you know the Way.
5   Thomas said to him:
    We do not know where you are going
    so how do we know the Way?

1   The House of God is the image of the Temple: the Sanctuary Tent in the desert, and the stone and cedar Temple in Jerusalem. And these, built with human hands, are the ritual signs of the true Dwelling of God, not a house like other houses.

A tangible *place* where God's Presence could be approached points to the obvious limit in human life. We dwell some *place* because we are dimensional beings. As our knowledge of our *place* expands we become strangely dislocated. A small portion of the surface of the earth with but vague feeling for what lies well beyond the horizon ("the ends of the earth") gives way to a world of continents and countless peoples. The earth as the center of creation and the dwelling place of its human rulers gives way to a universe of myriads of worlds and endless space, all mysteriously arising into existence through lengths of time we can represent in numbers but not imagine. In a universe of universes we begin to realize we cannot ultimately speak of a *place*, except in the small and constantly changing vision of a personal momentary place.

A *place* for God is our attempt to find God *with us* in our momentary place. He is in a Sanctuary or Temple, at a table or altar, on a mountain or within a hidden room, because *that is where we are*. The House of God is the sign of His true Dwelling: what it means to affirm HE IS, and what it means to know His Presence in the midst of human life. But House as a sign can confuse us. We can imagine that one place actually contains God in some way and so is inherently Holy Ground. Or we can imagine some "other" nonearthly place beyond our universe as a Heaven–place containing God. These are the dim images of "the old earth and old heavens" which are swept away as Christ makes everything *new*.

2   Thomas speaks within the limits of the old vision when he protests *we do not know* where *you are going so how do we know the* way? The image of the many–roomed house is that of a Sacred Palace with its many dwelling places of those who live with the King. For humble people with their tiny houses of one or two rooms, this is a symbol of glory indeed—to dwell with the King in his own home as his household–family. The Father's House is not "somewhere" and is not a house of rooms. It is the Living God Himself as He really dwells with us: One–with–us in Christ. Our simplest realization is absolutely true: wherever we are there God is. But although we inevitably speak in terms of place, "wherever. . .there", we must learn instead to recognize the *personal* reality: "we are. . .God is". The man Jesus

is the one in whom All–God–is dwells in Union. Jesus the Anointed–
with–God is the living Temple. This is the Temple not made by human
hands (Heb. 9:11), the Temple built of living stones (I Pet. 2:5), the Temple to be destroyed and restored in three days (Jn. 2:19).

Christ is not about to leave human life for some other "place"—a Heaven
where God dwells in a House. He is about to reveal the fullness of human
life: the Father dwells in the Son and in all who are drawn into the Son.
The House of God is the Living God alive in Christ and the many rooms
are the many persons coming to Life in him. They shall be with him where
he is.

> And the Word became flesh
> and raised his Sanctuary–Tent among us
> and we beheld his Glory. . .   (Jn. 1:14)

If we know "where" he is going, then we know the Way: Christ.

REVELATION IS CHRIST

John 14

6   I am the Way and the Truth and the Life—
     No one comes to the Father except through me.
7   If you had known me you would also have known my
     Father
     From this moment you both know Him and have seen
     Him.

1   Ancient peoples often spoke of their quest for experience of the Sacred
and the forming of a religious life in response to that experience as *The
Way*. It was as if they had discovered a road and it had only to be followed
to find the completion of life. The "walking" could be spoken of in terms
of matching footsteps to those of others who had gone before. The "pathway" was thought of as a pattern leading to the Sacred by means of precepts
or rituals or doctrines or mystic forms. The Mosaic Way of Torah, Lao Tzu's
mystical Way, Confucius' Way of Ritual, the Buddha's Middle Way, the Way
of the Gods of Shinto, the archaic Chant–way or Dance–way, Way of the

Forest, and all the others conceive of the Way always as some *thing*, a method, a principle. The earliest Christians were called "the followers of the Way". But their Way is a *person* not a *thing*.

I am the way—
no one comes to the Father except through me.

The Father is completely in Union in Christ His Son. He is in Union with the *complete* Christ, God–Man. Our human response (and it can only be human) to God enters this human reality of Christ. We can know and love another human being within *our* meaning of *know* and *love*. It is not an experience of reaching out abstractly to the Transcendence across the Void separating creatures and Creator, attempting to know and love the One we realize is Totally Other from us. We know and love God–in–Christ, One of *us*. We come within the fully human Jesus into that Union Father-and-Son. The Way is not a principle. He is the person we can come to know and love as persons, and suddenly awaken to *the Mystery he is*.

2   I am the Truth—
if you had known me, you also would have known my Father.

Once again, the Truth of Christ is not "truths"—things—it is his own living Self. This Truth cannot be taught in words or ideas. These can only alert us to him, pointing in his direction so that we can look and, hopefully, see. The first disciples had not been moved to ask what doctrines he taught, but rather where he lived. And he had called them to come and *learn him*.

Christ is the Truth, and the Truth we learn if we *learn him* is the Living God alive in human life. Not alive in some derivative sense—as Creator to be found reflected in His creatures, as an intervening Power reaching in to change what we are doing, or as a final Answer to our life-questions. The Living God is alive as an actual human being having taken to Himself true human nature and coming into our midst as one of us: born as human beings are and found in man's way of life (Phil. 2:7); to know the Father is not to know about the Father. Our words and ideas cannot present the Reality of God to us. Christ the Truth is the Presence. We do not know God in near-empty thoughts that merely hint at what we seek. We know God as we experience our own coming alive within Him.

3   *I am the Life—*
from this moment you both know Him and have seen Him.

Christ is our Life *now*, not in some distant future. The Living Temple
of the Father's Presence was about to be torn apart in the pouring out of
his life in death so others might live. But it has been restored, raised on
the Third Day in the triumph of Life. As the first disciples experienced
that Transformation and their re–creation in it, they realized that all had
been created New. As they moved more deeply within his Life they further realized that the living Seed of this renewal had been at the center
of existence from the very beginning:

> Through him all things came to be
> and without him not one existing thing came to be.
> In him was Life
> and the Life was the Light of men . . .
> That was the True Light
> Which enlightens everyone coming into the world.
>
> (Jn. 1:3-4, 9)

We seek God as the Living God because we experience what it means
to be alive. We do not impose the petty image of human life upon God.
God is Totally Other, *Totaliter Aliter*, in no way like us or any of creation.
God is no more a "living being" than He is a "force" or "principle". Yet
we affirm it is the Living God we know. As we live and seek the Sacred,
we seek as living beings. In our daily experience we are attracted to that
in the world which is more like us and can participate more fully in our
lives. We are alive, and we know the extraordinary power within whatever
lives. Throughout the universe the vast unliving energies and matter in
all its forms are indeed overwhelming to us. Yet we are truly moved when
we behold life, in even the smallest thing. For the power of life proclaims
the beginning of individuality and (ultimately for us) person—conscious
self, at that point when all energy and matter begins to be transcended.
We have been born from a lineage reaching back through all things to the
crudest "first", but we know we want to be free: free not to fall back and
be absorbed, *free to be*. We can experience at least the edge of that freedom.
Even within the limits of our born–life, we know we want *simply to be*. Life
urging us towards Transcendence–for–ourselves is the experience which

prompts us to speak of a *Living God*, not a "Principle" or "Cause" or any "Thing". We know our quest for Life turns us to Him and away from the ultimate lifelessness of mere universes. We are alive and must find a Living God.

If we can recognize Christ–the–Life we will realize we are seeing the Living God as He is, Father–to–us, in Whom our reborn–Life begins *at this moment* in our personal experience *who we are and are becoming*. To know and see the Father is by living, not by thinking. Ideas will inevitably take shape because of this living experience. But ideas themselves can never be the Life—Christ—in whom we come *to see* as we awaken more and more to the living.

SEEING GOD ALIVE

John 14

8   Philip said to him:
     Lord, show us the Father and that would satisfy us.
9   Jesus said to him:
     Have I been with you all this time, Philip,
     and still you have not known me?
     He who has seen me has seen the Father.
     So how can you say 'Show us the Father'?
10   Do you not believe
     I am in the Father and the Father is in me?
     The words I say to you I do not speak as from myself.
     But the Father living in me does His own works.
11   You must believe me as I say
     I am in the Father
     and the Father is in me.
     If for no other reason at least believe
     because of the works themselves.

1   Philip speaks for all of us. Without realizing it we are constantly betraying our own ambiguity as we seek to believe. We reduce our *experience* of Christ to *ideas about the experience* and concentrate our *minds* upon believing those *ideas*. Belief becomes a process of committing ourselves intellectually

to ideas, ideas always woefully incomplete and limited. Such belief ultimately becomes the acceptance of someone else's ideas simply on the external authority of a witness. The center of belief becomes the texts of the Scriptures or the statements of doctrine or the verbal truths of revelations. Christ the Way and the Truth and the Life is believed in as if these were ideas, and hence as if who he is and what he does are also ideas.

And so, with Philip, we want more than "belief"—*we want to see!* We want to *experience* the Reality of the Father ourselves, not just hear about Him. Christ's answer appeals to our experience: have we *really known* him or merely *known about* him? Is our experience nothing more than that of being stirred by the ideas of others who have represented Christ to us, or, beyond all such ideas, have we ourselves encountered the living Christ? Our own direct experience need not be insightful or deeply developed or well reflected upon to be real. As persons we encounter another person. The implications of personal encounters may be poorly grasped at first. But because it is the involvement of living persons, encounter can grow as they grow, from initial meeting through to the most transforming unity. This is the process we experience in our natural lives from birth: the newborn involved with another before any reflection is at all possible, growing to recognize and love as life is lived together. Knowledge takes a mental shape—thoughts, words—to give expression to our experience.

Have we been with Christ all this time and still do not really recognize him? Do images of Christ attract our attention away from personal recognition?

2   In the course of the Meal Christ will more and more insist on this recognition from within our actual unity with him. We recognize him as we recognize ourselves–with–him. We see him in, through and with us as together we are *completely one.* And this recognition of him is as he is: a human being in living Union with the Fullness of God—and we ourselves drawn into unity with him and so into that living Union. Whoever *sees* Christ *sees* the Father. If we actually do experience Christ we are experiencing the Father in our own direct experience. But this is not the experience of an external encounter. It is not approaching near or coming into the Presence of God. It is our own entering into the living Union who is Christ. To believe is to experience this: Christ in the Father and the Father in Christ. There is no God "somewhere else" yet to be seen. In Christ we see the Glory, and we see Christ as we see ourselves alive in his unity.

Christ's words, *I am in the Father and the Father is in me*, are not to be taken as the signs of ideas but of the works of the Father living in him. They proclaim "see what He is doing" not "understand what this means". The work of the Father is Creation, the creation of Life.

> For this is the Will of my Father:
> that everyone who sees the Son
> and believes in him
> shall have Eternal Life.   (Jn. 6:40)
> I have come so that they may have Life
> and have it to the full.   (Jn. 10:10)

One cannot be alive and not experience being alive. We can think about life only if life is ours. We believe because we see, because we experience we are alive with him. The work of the Father is the giving of His Life to us through His Son as Christ gives us his unitive Life. If we have been reborn into this Life we ourselves see the Father, from *within Him*.

GROWING CHRIST LIFE

John 14

12   Amen! Amen! I say to you:
      He who believes in me
      will do the same works I myself do,
      and he will do even greater works than these,
      because I am going to the Father.
13   And whatever you ask in my Name
      I will do it
      so that the Father may be glorified in the Son.
14   If you ask me anything in my Name
      I will do it.

1   To believe is to live in Christ, experiencing coming into the Life he gives. This Life is not a perfect human life. Human life as such cannot be perfect in any real sense, for it is the limited existence of each already circumscribed individual person. Eternal Life is not an endless limited life merely evading death. The Life given in Christ is the inmost Reality of

God. We receive into ourselves the Power through His Spirit for our inner selves to grow—transform—

and thus know that which surpasses knowledge:
the Love of Christ—
so that you may be filled
with the entire Fullness of God.   (Eph. 3:19)

In the gift of Life we receive the Whole God, not merely an effect from God. And therefore in Christ we begin to do the same re-creative work of Life-giving. We can know from within the meaning of *belief* because we give the Life we have received. As we learn from our Teacher and Lord that *God serves us*, so unitively in Christ *God—we serve still others.*

It is the same work, yet it is even greater since it continues to grow as the human reality of Christ grows, drawing in more and more persons, constantly extending the Incarnation: God in Union with One Man in Union with countless men and women, encompassing the full human family. As each person awakens to the Life given, each further gives. And as the giving is not giving a *thing* but the Living God Himself, the human work grows greater in its unity. The Seed of Life is born in Jesus the Only-Begotten, who plants himself in others, in whom he grows rooted in Love, and all together reach out to grasp the breadth and length and height and depth of all that exists (Eph. 3:17–19).

2   The Power of Life has come forth from the Father in His Son, entering human life, to transform us. Christ-with-us returns into the Father and we are One. Human life is transformed without being destroyed. We live as persons still growing, reaching out and discovering ourselves, yet also, mysteriously, we know the Gift has already been given.

We ask in his Name, "name" in its ancient significance: that inner principle of selfhood whereby a person actually exists as *this person. To seek in the Name of Christ is to seek in his own reality, to seek as he actually is.* He is Christ-with-us, not "someone else". If we ask with this realization we will find we are not asking for *things* but are seeking to live ever more deeply the Life given in Christ and seeking to further give that Life. And *Christ will do it* and *the Father will be glorified in the Son.*

INDWELLING SPIRIT

John 14

15 If you love me
    you will keep my commandments.
16 And I will ask the Father
    and He will give you another Helper
    to be with you forever:
17 the Spirit of Truth
    whom the world cannot receive
    because it neither sees nor knows Her.
18 You know Her
    because She dwells in you
    and is in you.

1   For the community of John the Torah was not the prefiguring of a more perfect pattern for life to come in Christ. The pattern of commands given in the Torah was itself a perfect pattern. But it was a pattern for humans who were being drawn towards a purely human perfection. It could not envision that our destiny was to transcend the creature–only, and being transformed to receive the Gift of God Himself. There can be no pattern or method of living to achieve such a transformation, to be alive within the Living God, completely One with Him. This can only occur by His free Self–giving. It can only occur because *He loves* and *we Love* in response. Torah did not pass away, nor was it abolished by being finally fulfilled. Torah as the pattern for human life underwent the same Transformation into Life as did those who received the Gift of Life.

Jesus had taught that the two–fold command of Love—God and neighbor—was the norm for perceiving the meaning of all the commands of the Torah. At first this would be understood by the disciples simply as the principle for interpreting the other commands and putting them into practice. But they were to discover he was giving a new commandment: love not merely within the limits of the human acts of love, but love in the very act of Love Who God is. Receive God, be transformed by this Gift into Union within God, and now give *This*. Love God with that Love with which the Son loves the Father, and love others with that Love with which the Father loves the Son. If we love Christ with *This* we will keep his commandments of Love. It is no longer a pattern of life that we seek to live. We are transformed to live Life Itself and the true Torah is transformed with us so that we recognize *he is the Truth*.

We know we are alive in God because we experience *we have changed*. However dimly we see or poorly we understand, we know we recognize *God in His Son in us*. And this is not our own creation, it is not an idea or wish. We find ourselves to be *different*, recognizing ourselves in this new identity we share in Christ. Since it is a new Life, the change—rebirth—is spoken of in the ancient image of life: spirit, *the breath of life*. We enter and share the living identity of the Son by being born again through the Spirit. We were born once through the flesh and so are in bodily life; we are reborn through the Spirit and so are in the Life which is Spirit.

2   God gives Himself to us, and so becomes *our* Father, in a dual process of Life which we experience. We experience God *Giving* and God *Given*. God *Given* is the *One* Who comes forth—True God from True God: the Son, the True Image, the Divinity Incarnate in Jesus the Anointed. God *Giving* is the *Coming forth* as One—Living Unity: the Spirit, the Inmost Power, the Anointing Unification of all into Christ. The *Giving* and the *Given* are experienced in our Transformation as the Paracletes, the Ones Who as One are our Helpers, re–creating us into new Life. In the image of human parenthood, God Giving as the Spirit is in the image of mother, the one through Whom we are *reborn* into the Life *begotten* (the image of father) by the Son.

Our affirmation of Spirit as the experienced Life–giving is the new Truth we are living as we share the identity of the Son. He and we become truly One through the Power of the Spirit. It is the Power through which we come alive and so our image of Spirit is Mother.

> How can a grown man be reborn?
> Can he enter his mother's womb again and be reborn?
> Amen! Amen! I say to you:
> unless one is born through water and the Spirit
> he cannot enter the Kingdom of God—
> what is born of the flesh is flesh,
> what is born of the Spirit is Spirit.   (Jn. 3:4-6)

The Spirit is our Mother at the moment of our new birth, when with our first cry of Life we recognize who we have become and so recognize the Truth of God.

> And because you are offspring God has sent forth
> the Spirit of His Son into our hearts
> crying out: *Abba!—Father!*   (Gal. 4:5–6)

3   The experience of John's community included the baffling rejection of the Gift in Christ. They could not understand how this can happen (—even if, in the end, it *finally* does happen). They *see* and *know* the Spirit because they have received the Gift and realize it. Of those who seem to reject they can only say the obvious: those neither *see* nor *know*, they fail to recognize.

All awakened to Life recognize the Spirit because they experience Her. It is the Spirit *sent into our hearts* in Whom we cry out *Abba!—Father!* The heart, at the center of our life–blood, is the symbol of the center of our living personhood, our own spirit. The Spirit *dwells in us and is in us— within* in the deepest sense. This is our actual experience:

> you received a Spirit of adoption
> by which we cry out *Abba!—Father!*.
> The Spirit Herself bears witness
> together with our own spirit
> that we are children of God.   (Rm. 8:15–16)

LIVING UNION

John 14

18   I will not leave you orphans,
        I am returning to you.
19   In a little while the world will no longer see me,
        but you will see me
        for I live and you will live.
20   On that day you will realize:

I in my Father,
and you in me,
and I in you!

21   Whoever receives my commandments and keeps them
is the one who loves me,
and whoever loves me
will be loved by my Father
and I will love him
and will show myself to him.

1   Once again Christ affirms the experience of his presence, not absence. In the earlier image of the Father's House with its many rooms he spoke of taking the disciples to the "place" where the Father dwells. Now the promise of his living presence is personal: the Father's dwelling–place is not a *place* but *people*.

We are brought to Life in our rebirth in Christ through the Spirit. We truly are the offspring of God. And we shall never be abandoned as orphans, given Life only to be left to die.

Within the space of a few hours the human life of Christ underwent the awesome *change* of dying–and–rising into the Fullness of Life. We can realize something of the vastness of that change as we reflect on our own experience of human life: how can any of us, so clearly limited, expect to receive the Fullness of God into ourselves? Obviously we cannot as presently constituted within our limited lives. And if Jesus of Nazareth is a human being as we are he cannot either—unless human life can be reconstituted, made a new creation, be so totally changed that life can become Life. In his Transformation through dying–and–rising Christ can no longer be seen by "the world", *the untransformed*, but those who share in the Transformation will see him as he *now* is. This is not a matter of being "blinded" and unable to see with our eyes. Nor is it an apparition or vision or anything of the like for those who will see. And it is not an act of committed faith in which there is "belief" in spite of no "seeing".

To see Christ is *to live*, not to look: *You will see me for I live and you will live*. He is speaking of the radically transformed Life he–we experience, life–into–Life, not merely human life reestablished and improved following natural death. Only those who live *as he is now alive* can perceive him in his full Presence. For that living Presence is Son–in–Father, we–in–him and he–in–us. The Son–in–Father (and hence Christ and ourselves interdwelling) is the inner Unity of God in Himself manifested in the Christ

Union God–Man, re–creating humanity to be able to receive the Godhead. The inner Son–in–Father is not a visual object to be experienced as sight. He is the Living God, and we can only experience our Union by living.

2   Again, experiencing this Life is identified in the experience of living in Love. To receive and keep the commandment is to respond in Love to Christ and, being loved by the Father, *I will Love, and show myself*. The completing experience of loving—any love, even the narrowest—is the realization of a union. Human love in all its forms is a unity of what otherwise would be separate: possessive love, *eros*, one possessing or possessed by another; bonded love, *phile*, of those responding to being related, as parents and children, brothers and sisters, friends; selfless love, *agape*, opening to others in giving rather than taking, and a giving which forms relationship rather than responds to relationships already constituted. To experience love is to realize union. For Christ to promise his Love, *Agape*, is the promise of Union, and as we experience the process of growing into One in him we begin to perceive him: know him, recognize him *as he is now*.

THE GIVING SPIRIT

John 14

23   If anyone loves me
he will keep my word
and my Father will love him
and We will come to him
and make Our home with him.
24   He who does not love me
does not keep my words.
And the word you hear is not mine
but is that of the Father Who sent me.
25   These things I have spoken to you
while still with you
but the Helper, the Holy Spirit,
26   Whom the Father will send in my Name
will teach all to you
and remind you of all
which I have told you.

1   The disciple Jude does not grasp the significance of how Christ is about to reveal himself. He represents all who fail to realize the difference between *seeing* and *recognizing* Christ. The Gospel community is aware that Faith can be thought of merely in terms of believing the testimony of others who are trusted as witnesses. We can "believe" in the sense of trusting that others have "seen" though we have not. We can put confidence in *words* in the hope that one day we ourselves will experience. Jesus answers how it is that he is about to show himself to disciples but not to the world as he gives a deeper meaning to *word*.

Keeping Christ's word does not consist in accepting a new Torah with new commandments, or a body of doctrines or ideas. Christ's word is not his but the Father's, and the Father's Word is Christ himself. Ancient peoples might imagine God as possessing truths or wisdom to be imparted to us in words; they thought of the prophets as speaking "God's word" or message, and of the Torah given as the earthly mirror–image of a heavenly wisdom. But the *words* are ours, as we form our consciousness in response to the Mystery of God. God's Presence can be felt at the very center of every moment of creation, and each time we are made aware of this Reality we are moved to attempt to grasp the *real* meaning of ourselves, of what we are thinking and doing, and of the world of our experience. Of course God does not speak words or possess a mind streaming with ideas. The speech and thought are ours and take shape in us as we move deeply within God.

2   *The word you hear is not mine but is that of the Father Who sent me.* Christ is the Only Word of God: he alone as Son comes forth from within the Father, he alone is the True Image who does not "represent" God but is himself the Presence. The Word of God is not a thing, but a Person. The most the ancients could imagine was an illuminating message coming from God in words which could be learned. The Reality revealed in Christ is the unique Living Word. He cannot be learned (merely thought about, understood). As with any person, we can *really know* only by the experience of living unitively, by loving. *If anyone Loves me he will keep my word. . .* To love is to share one's self with another, and if the love is completed both selves are shared in a living unity: . . .and my Father will love him, and We will come to him and make Our home with him.

The Father sends the Spirit in the Name of Christ, in the continuing personal presence of Christ. It is the Life–giving Spirit, the *Giving* in Whom we receive the Reality of the Son *Given* to us to be our own Life. This Spirit *teaches* us *to recognize* all Christ is, the Christ–with–us. All he said is *brought to mind* as we recognize him, and as we grow in that recognition we come to understand more and more. We seek to put into words the meaning of the Living Word Whom we experience. Through the Gift of the Spirit we are taught *from within*, taught by living and reflecting upon the experience of that living.

It has been written in the prophets:
And they shall all be taught by God.
Anyone who hears and learns from the Father
comes to me.   (Jn. 6:45)

The Father loves and comes to anyone who comes in love to the Son. With such a one They make Their home.

WHOLENESS IN CHRIST

John 14

27   Peace I leave you,
  my peace I give you.
  Not as the world gives it
  do I give it to you.
  Do not let your hearts be troubled or afraid.
28   You have heard what I told you:
  I am going away
  and shall return to you.
  If you loved me
  you would have rejoiced
  that I am going to the Father
  for the Father is greater than I.
29   And now I have told you before it happens
  that when it does happen you may believe.
30   I shall not speak with you much longer
  for the Principle of this world is coming
  and since it has no power over me

31   the world will therefore know
I love the Father,
and do just as the Father has commanded me.

1   The peace of Christ is not the courteous greeting exchanged in count-less everyday meetings. His is the Gift of Peace. It is *Shalom* in its root mean-ing of whole, perfect and undivided, *shalem*. The Peace Christ gives is his *whole self*, in whom lives the undivided One God, and in whom we come alive in the perfect Union. In this Peace we can live at the very heart of the final struggle of life–and–death into which we all must enter as we die and rise in Christ. He goes through death, returning to take us with him into Life. In this Peace we find the cause of our joy.

The True Image has come forth from within the Father into human life, the Son alive as an actual man, God–and–Man made Whole. In our Spirit rebirth in the Son this Incarnation is opened to become God–and–Man–and–men/women made Whole. As our response of love completes the Union we are in Christ, we rejoice: we are the One going to the Father! We experience it has already begun to happen and so we believe.

Through baptism
we were buried–together–with him in his death
so that as Christ was raised from among the dead
through the Glory of the Father
so we also might walk in the newness of Life.
. . .
If we died with Christ
we believe we also shall live–together–with him,
realizing that Christ having been raised from among the dead
never again dies,
never again does death have power over him.   (Rm. 6:4, 8–9)

2   The world will know the meaning of Christ's love of the Father as Christ loves all given him by the Father to the end, completely, doing just as the Father commands. We experience this Whole Love, and so believe.

For I am convinced:
not death, not life,

not angels, not rulers, nothing already existing,
nothing yet to come,
not powers,
neither height nor depth,
nor any other creature
shall be able to separate us
from the Love of God made visible
in Christ Jesus our Lord.   (Rm. 8:38–39)

FRUITFUL CHRIST LIFE

John 15

1   I am the true vine
     and my Father is the vinedresser.
2   Every branch in me which does not bear fruit
     He cuts away
     and every branch which does bear fruit
     He prunes
     so it may bear more fruit.
3   You are already pruned
     through the word which I have spoken to you.
     Dwell in me,
     and I in you!
4   As the branch cannot bear fruit by itself
     but only if it dwells in the vine
     neither can you unless you dwell in me.
5   I am the vine,
     you are the branches.
     He who dwells in me and I in him
     bears much fruit,
     but separated from me
     you can do nothing.
6   Unless one dwells in me
     he would be like a branch
     cast aside and withered—
     these are gathered up

and thrown into the fire and burned.

7   If you dwell in me
and my words dwell in you
then ask whatever you desire
and it shall come to you.

8   In this is my Father glorified
that you bear much fruit
and then you will be my disciples.

1   The image of the vine is a double expression of the living Christ: as
he is alive he brings forth more life, and he is the complete unity of himself
and all those alive in him. He is the true vine of his Father, not the vine
spoken of in Isaiah (5:1) and Jeremiah (2:21), the vine planted by God in
His own land but which brought forth only sour fruit and whose offshoots
withered.

We realize that something is alive as we see it generating new life. The
power of life is not identified merely with internal activities or even the
ability to draw in and assimilate elements from outside. Life is powerful
because it is creative. A living thing is so independent it can make more
independent things from within itself! The more complex living things—
more complex and so more independent and so more powerful—create new
individuals which are not simply duplications of themselves. Their offspring
can be very different from them, can become greater than their parents.
And, finally, beings can be given life who are so independent and so powerful that they can turn to one another, giving–and–receiving one another
and thus create a new power of life: love.

The Son is the true vine of the Father, coming forth from within the
Life Power of the Father and loving Him in perfect Unity. This living Christ
gives this Life to all who dwell in him. And they are alive as they in turn
bring forth this Life.

2   The image of the vine restates the mystery of response: the unfruitful
are dead, to be cut away from the living, while the fruitful are alive and
are to be drawn ever deeper into life by the pruning away of everything
but the most powerful center of themselves. The mystery of response is not
(cannot) be resolved in this image—why are branches fruitful or fruitless?
But perhaps we can become more sensitive to the fact that we are speaking of *living persons* in the figure of branches, not *things* which we can
imagine as dead, useless, fit for destruction.

People are purified—drawn deeper into the already–given Christ Life—through the Word Who is Christ. He is not a "word of judgment" as so often spoken by the prophets in condemnation. He is the Word Who brings Life to the dead, saving the lost. He brings Life not by speaking words of wisdom, commands or truths, but by being the Life himself and in his recreative Power re–conceiving us so we can be reborn. This is the Gift for all, the just and unjust alike, and any who continue to dwell in him, their new Source, will continue to live, eventually bearing fruit themselves as they are purified.

They are purified as they move from the possibility (or actuality) of inner dividedness toward ever greater wholeness, as the center of their lives as persons becomes more and more open to unity. What is "pruned away" is the nonunitive, the destructive, all that divides us within ourselves and from others. We can mistake this process as negative: cutting some reality out of ourselves or separating us from persons, things or relationships which otherwise would interfere with some imagined purity. On the contrary, it is a positive process allowing more profound involvements. The natural figure of pruning branches actually suggests a purification by concentrating the innate power of the living member: the branch could grow in many directions with several shoots each sapping the strength of all as they work against each other dissipating—dividing—the creative power ready to bring forth fruit. The vinedresser keeps the branch whole and undivided by con-centrating its new growth in its single strongest thrust, and it brings forth an abundance of new life instead of fruitless shoots doomed to wither.

3   The word of Christ which purifies us is his revealing command: *dwell in me, and I in you!* It is the command *Live!* But it cannot be fulfilled by obedience, for to have the Life of Christ as he gives Life we must love as we are loved—*you in me, I in you* It is not really a command, a demand that we do something. It is the Revelation who is Christ: the Living God so loves us He gives Himself in His Son to be our Life so we can love. If we do dwell in him then the greatest Life Power wells up within us and we turn to one another giving–and–receiving that Love Who is God. Only in this is there ultimate fruitfulness, as this New Life is born in more and more and more.

God alone is Glorious, He alone is the Power of Life. As the Son manifests that Power by bringing us into Life the Father is glorified. This is not an external adulation, the superficial praise we think of as giving glory. The Father is glorified as the Life He *is* is given: in the Son to us.

But if it truly is the ultimate Power of Life we receive, we must come fully into that Life and ourselves be able to beget new Life in still others. It is the actual creativity of life–begetting which alone manifests the Power and so alone glorifies the Father.

The inner Glory of the Father is not merely represented in a created image; it is not the natural human power of life hinting at the True Life. The inner Glory is directly experienced in receiving–and–giving the Living God. To be abundantly fruitful is to give Glory, and in this we become true disciples—alive ourselves and making others to live. And this is the final answer to all we ask for ourselves and all others: what we really desire, whatever the form or circumstances of our askings, is nothing less than the very Life of God as our own. It is ours, and in this is the Father—*our* Father—glorified.

DWELLING IN LOVE

John 15

9   Just as the Father has loved me
so I have loved you.
Dwell in my Love.

10   If you keep my commandments
you will dwell in my Love,
just as I have kept my Father's commandments
and so dwell in His Love.

11   I have spoken these things to you
so that my joy may be in you
and your joy may be made full.

12   This is my commandment:
that you love one another
as I have loved you.

1   For the third time the Gospel community recalls the giving of the new commandment of Love: we are to live in the Love which is the inner Union of Father and Son. In living this Love the disciples will be recognized to be who they really are in Christ (13:35), the Spirit will be given so that the disciples can awaken in the New Life to see the risen Christ (14:16,21),

and they will experience the joyous Christ in his gift of joy.

Over and over the earliest communities stress that the basis of their *belief* is their actual *experience*. They do not *believe about* Christ, they *believe in* him. They know Christ alive after dying because they themselves have encountered him. Here they speak of this in the experience of deep personal joy, the joy which flows within us when we are unitively present with one we love.

Christ is the joyous Christ because he is the Son dwelling in the Father, and they are completely One. Father and Son are not merely unitively present with one another, coming *into* love. This is the Mystery: God IS Love. Two individuals are not being unified into one. This *is* the Oneness, the Hidden God absolutely present, fully Given and known by us in Christ. The joy of Christ is this inner living in Love. This is the joy given to us.

2   Our unity in Christ is two–fold. We are unitively present with one another in personal love. As human beings he and we are drawn into unity. But the one we come to know and love is the one who dwells in the Father, the one in whom the Fullness of God dwells incarnate. Our experience of love is thus two–fold: in the single act of love we love as *individual persons* who are *unitively within* the Love Who is God. Our experience of joy flows from this Christ Love: we are joyous as persons–together within the Oneness Given to us. His joy is given to us so that our joy may be made full. The Mystery of the Fullness of God is revealed to us as in Christ we live in the experience of *this* joy—not that we grasp its meaning, rather we are grasped by it: we recognize Christ–and–ourselves joyous.

Our *experience* of Faith is as complex as we are. At our center we are transformed to receive God as He is. We awaken in consciousness to this Gift in many ways. We come to recognize Christ (in many ways) alive in our lives. We respond as whole persons, in spirit, mind and body. We move in the powers flowing within us—our peace, our freedom, our joy. All of these together are our one experience of Christ. Each is a moment in our experience which bears witness: *it is true!* We believe because we have seen—and we know we see because we ourselves experience.

Whatever it ultimately means to say *the Father loves the Son*, that is the Love Given to us: *just as the Father has loved me so I have loved you*. And it is that Love we must share together: *love one another as I have loved you*. Because we dwell in that Love we can know full joy, joy deeper than the crises which can grip us: unresolveable tensions, failures of justice and goodness, the erosion of life, and the seeming destruction at death. It is Easter Joy: Christ is alive! It is Gospel Joy: We are alive!

MINISTRY OF LOVE

John 15

13   No one has greater love than this:
    that he lay down his life for his friends.
14   You are my friends
    if you do what I command you.
15   No longer do I call you servants
    for the servant does not know
    what his master is doing.
    But I have called you friends
    because I have made known to you
    everything I have heard from the Father.
16   You did not choose me,
    but I have chosen you
    and have commissioned you
    to go forth and bear fruit
    and your fruit will endure—
    for the sake of it
    whatever you ask the Father in my Name
    He will give you.
17   This I command you:
    love one another.

1   We readily recognize the greatest act of human love in the willing sacrifice of one's life for the sake of another. It is beyond possessing and being possessed in love; it is beyond the bonding relationships of the love experienced in sharing. This is the love which *gives*, gives to the point of death, and the one who thus loves is beyond possession and bond. We can accept this love and respond deeply to the one who loves us so. But such a love cannot be simply returned: the giving is final and so the giver is gone (gone but not lost!).

To lay down human life for another is not to give one's *self*, but to give up the power of life in the bodily world which brought us into existence and in the world of persons with whom we have grown to become ourselves. We are unable to give our actual selfhood to another, we can only *give of* our selves. We can give up life, allowing death, allowing ourselves to be killed in such a way that it is a choice (not the usual mere inevitability), a choice which becomes our final gift to another. But the unique person each of us is cannot be given away to another. Personal uniqueness is precisely that: there is no other *in any way* like *me* in my inmost self–identity. Uniqueness is mysterious, even to the self–reflective person himself—it is not a "thing" among other things, it is not an "element" in our constitution; it is the very center of identity *who each is*. The unique person as such cannot be reduced to a possession of another or to a relationship with another. The selfhood cannot be given away. The person who gives all that can be given is still that same unique person, gone from the living world but not lost, no longer alive (in the basic experience of natural human life) but not destroyed.

2   When we recognize the willing giving of one's life as the act of *love* we are affirming our inner conviction that in death the *person* is not destroyed. Otherwise to give one's life for another would be truly meaningless. If the inmost self were simply identifiable with world and body and relationship, and perishable with them, why give one's moment of life to another who really cannot profit from it since all are equally hurrying to destruction? And if the gift is made nonetheless as heroic tragedy, why call it *love* and not simply sentiment, irrational emotion, instinct or the like? For when we speak of *love* we express our experience of creativity, life–giving, fostering deeper existence—not the momentary delay of destruction. The greatest love we know, giving up life for one we love, is not the greatest act of despair buying only one more hopeless hour before the end! We somehow know that in their ultimate significance *love* and *person* are the same mystery, unique and so undefinable. In this mystery we are affirming our awareness that where we find a person loving completely we realize (without understanding or proving it) *person* cannot be lost.

Those who were his Christ loved to the end completely. He gave his life so they could live. This is a two–fold giving: the laying down of his human life as a free choice; but in him lives the Fullness of God and so That is given to us in his greatest Love. The inmost selfhood of Christ and the Selfhood of God are unitively One, and thus when Jesus *gives of himself* in laying down his life he gives God *Himself*. The greatest human act of love becomes in Christ the only possible divine act of love. God, absolutely One, has no–thing to give us: He IS Himself, and His Self becomes our Gift. We neither possess God nor are possessed by God; we are not merely in relationship with God. God is Love—God is Given: God–and–Jesus One, God–and–Jesus–and–all One.

3   As he gives this Love we become friends, no longer servants. For the Johannine community this moment of change embraces several meanings, each leading us deeper into our identity with Christ.

First, it is the change in the relationship of disciple with master, in which the disciple himself becomes a master. On the first day of the public ministry, disciples of John the Baptist were sent by their master to Jesus as the one for whom John had been preparing them. Their first word to Jesus—Rabbi-Teacher—signaled their expectation: they sought him out as their new Master, the one who would lead them into Truth, and so they became his disciples. The master–disciple relationship always has one final purpose, to raise up new masters. It is a life–giving, life–nurturing process. The religious master seeks to impart not only knowledge but, more important, wisdom—living Truth. And in his ministry to them the disciples grow into that maturity which will enable them in their turn to be masters ministering the living Truth to still others. The master–disciple relationship is not a permanent condition but a generative process known by its fruitfulness: at one point disciples cease to be disciples, becoming masters in their own right and colleagues—friends—with the one who has been their master.

In the vision of ancient Israel elders had been raised up by God's choice to assist Moses in guiding the people in their understanding of Torah and in settling their disputes and obligations under Torah (Num. 11:16,ff.) To these was imparted a portion of the Spirit which was upon Moses and through which he was Leader of the covenanted people. Throughout the history of Israel there was a succession to this original eldership of the seventy–two, each elder gathering disciples and, when they had matured in the wisdom of Torah to be able themselves to *teach* and *judge*, the disciples were ordained masters by their masters, who *imparted the Spirit to them* (note Jn. 20:22). They were now fellow masters and friends to their master, and elders in Israel bringing the living wisdom of Torah to the people and seeking out the next generation of disciples to become masters.

4   The disciples of Christ are no longer servants but friends if they do what he has commanded—living by the Wisdom he is, living in the commandment of Love. He calls them friends because he has taught them everything he himself has received from the Father. They are now masters with their master for he chose them, raised them to their present maturity, and now they are to go forth and bear fruit that will endure. They will do the same works he does—Life-giving—but it is to be ever greater as generation after generation the Life who is Christ is extended, drawing more and more into the Union of God-and-Man-and-all.

The disciples are servants no longer because they now begin to realize "servant" has a new meaning in Christ. They do not serve him, he serves them. To serve is not human servility but God serving us, giving Himself. Served by God, receiving this Gift, they now can serve *This* to others. Christ has revealed himself to be not the Servant of God, but the Serving God, and those who become actively One with him participate in this Service. To serve as God serves is to give the Living God as He is Given, in Christ: to respond in love to the Love Who makes us truly One, by loving others with All we are—to lay down life for friends.

For the sake of those to whom we seek to bring Christ Life, the Father will give anything we ask in the Name of Christ. We ask in the Name—Identity—of Christ when we actually share his Identity, are One with him. When we ask as Christ asks, we desire one thing only: that all may have Life and have Life in its Fullness. We wish to give what we have received.

The first disciples had asked *Rabbi, where do you live?* They lived with him and grew into his Wisdom, and now could teach the transforming commandment: *This I command you: Love one another.*

MYSTERY OF REJECTION

John 15

18   If the world hates you
 realize it has hated me before you.
19   If you were of the world
 the world would have loved its own.
 But as you are not of the world
 since I chose you drawing you from the world

therefore the world hates you.

20   Remember the word I said to you:
the servant is not greater than his master.
If they persecuted me
they will persecute you also,
if they kept my word
they will keep yours also.

21   But they will do all these things to you
because of my Name
for they do not know the One Who sent me.

22   Unless I had come and spoken to them
they would not have sinned
but now they have no excuse for their sin.

23   He who hates me also hates my Father.

24   If I had not done works among them
such as no other man has ever done
they would not have sinned.
But now they have both seen and hated
both me and my Father.

1   The mystery of good and evil is centered in persons, not in things.
Love, life and giving flow to persons. Hatred, death and rejection grip persons. It is Christ the living person who is God Given to us in Love, and
we respond and receive this Gift, and so *love one another*. To hate another
is to refuse to receive. How can someone actually reject the One–All Who
alone really IS? Can anyone ultimately reject? We must discover in Christ
that we cannot ask these questions. We can only reflect the experience
of this mystery in our own moments of Christ Life—freely Given in Love
to all, to those who accept and to those who seem to reject.

2   God in Christ came and spoke and did the work of Life–giving, and
people he loved would turn on him in hatred—sin without excuse. Yet he
would give nonetheless, and continue to give in, through and with all those
who do accept and become One in him. And so the disciples–become–
friends come and speak and do the works of Life–giving, and are warned
that they shall share in the full mystery of Christ: Love unconditionally
given and never withdrawn even in the face of hatred—Life transcending
death. Only in this can we bear the fruit that will endure, and thus be

friends, true disciples, branches alive in the Vine of our Father.

SPIRIT OF TRUTH

John 15

26 When the Helper comes
    Whom I will send you from the Father—
    the Spirit of Truth
    Who comes forth from the Father—
    She shall bear witness to me.
27 And you also shall bear witness
    for you have been with me from the beginning.
    . . .

John 16

8   And when She comes
    She will bring conviction to the world
    about sin and justice and judgment—
9   sin: in that they did not believe in me,
10 justice: in that I am going to the Father
    and you see me no longer,
11 judgment: in that the reigning principle of this world
    has been condemned.

1   The witness to the reality of Christ is to be found neither in signs and wonders nor in a natural wisdom of the mind. The fact of God in Christ cannot be proved by any argument or evidence, for it is the Living God fully alive in Christ—it is *the fact of personhood* and this can only be known by direct experience person–with–person. Christ did not come to reveal things, but the True God in his Person. Therefore it is from within the inmost living Selfhood of God that the True Witness comes forth: the Spirit, the Life–Center of God. If we personally encounter God Himself in Christ then we know the Truth. Such personal encounter is possible only if the inner Giving Spirit comes to transform us, to bring us into the Life of God through rebirth so that by experiencing we can know we share His Identi-

ty. The transforming Spirit bears witness as in the Spirit we awaken in our New Life, and this rebirth is the beginning of our witness to Christ—the Fullness dwelling bodily in us his members as we are together the One Christ.

2   This True Witness in the Spirit reveals the complete mystery of Christ, the Divine Giving and the human response with its two free possibilities of acceptance or rejection. As the Spirit comes in Transformation people freely divide. It is this division which itself is the conviction of sin, of judgment and of justice. This is a radically different realization of conviction from that spoken of by the ancient prophets. They saw sin as disobedience to a Will of God expressed first in human conscience and finally in the gift of Torah. Justice was to be achieved in obedience to this Will. Judgment would be the act of God rewarding justice and punishing sin. But the coming of the Spirit is the moment in which the world is convicted because "the world" are those who reject and so divide themselves from Christ their only Life. The first disciples at the Paschal Meal were promised that the Spirit would come shortly, as Christ returned within the Glory of the Father. The conviction is thus already accomplished and is a part of the living witness of each generation reborn through the Spirit.

3   Sin is the refusal to believe. But this is not a willful act of the mind, a refusal to accept truths revealed. *They did not believe in me.* This is the rejection of a person, not a thing. As such it is not an act of the mind, willfully disobeying a precept or principle. It is hatred, as hatred is opposed to love. To love is to accept another, to embrace and receive another into one's own personal life, to become one together. The Spirit brings the world to the conviction of sin as we all recognize we can reject others, repulse and exclude them from life, become divided against one another. This sin is not the rejection of the *idea* of Christ but of Christ as he fully is:

> If anyone says: I love God
> and hates his brother
> he is a liar!
> For he who does not love his brother
> whom he has seen
> cannot love God
> whom he has not seen.   (I Jn. 4:20)

4   Justice is the return into the Glory of the Father. Justice had been conceived of as a life conforming to Divine Will, the obedience to Torah and faithfulness to Covenant. It was a human condition and destiny in which natural fulfillment would be realized. The justice of God the All–Just would be mirrored in the blessed life of the just man who lived meditating on and taking delight in all that came forth from the mouth of God. But as the Spirit brings the conviction of Christ's justice to the world, we find justice is not a human state. It is not a life of obedience or faithfulness, nor of moral balances. And it is not our imagination of an All–Just God as a source of laws and commands regulating life in accord with an eternal pattern.

Justice is Christ in Glory, the human embodying the Self of God Himself. Rather than faithful conformity to God, justice in Christ is the integral Union in God. It is God beyond our imagination of an All–Just source of what humans should *do*: it is the God in Whom we *are*. We were puzzled by the question whether or not anyone could really be just, be faithful in responding obedience and actually live justified to God. In the Spirit we realize this is a meaningless question. All the acts and conditions of human life which we too simply identify as justice must be recognized as flowing from the one who is just, the One dwelling in Glory. It is Glory beyond imagined justice, the Glory which *is* God, the God Who reveals Himself to be Love, the Love beyond imagined justice.

> And if you know that He is just
> know also that everyone who practices justice
> has been born of Him.
> Behold what manner of Love
> the Father has given us
> that we may be called children of God—
> and we are!   (I Jn. 2:29, 3:1)

We are swept into our own participation in the living mystery of Christ —he brings us unitively with him as he enters through dying–and–rising into the Glory of Union. *I am going to the Father, and you see me no longer.* But he goes to prepare our place with him so we can dwell together with him. He can be seen no longer outside the Life of Glory—Love—and neither can those alive in him. Therefore, who they *are* (God Given) and what they *do* (Giving God) cannot be accepted by a rejecting world.

5   Judgment has already been given: the reigning principle of the rejecting world has been condemned. The True Witness of the Spirit within
all the living witnesses reveals the triumph of the Life of Love over death.
God's Self–gift in Christ has already been Given, we have been joined to
him in his loving laying down of life, and joined in his rising into New Life.

> Therefore the world does not know us
> because it did not know him.
> Beloved, now we are children of God
> and it has not yet been shown
> what we shall be.   (I Jn. 3:2)

Living our transformed lives we day by day move toward the completion of our growth into the ultimate perfection of Christ, but we are the
offspring of God *now!* We still must become What he is, but we are fully
alive in Christ Life now. And so the judgment that convicts the world is
not a single event someday in the future "at the end"; it is the ongoing
condemnation of the principle of death. Love actually lived is the daily
condemnation of the attempt to possess, control and dominate others, rejecting them from our lives, killing them in countless ways.

> Do not wonder, brothers, if the world hates you.
> We know we have passed from death to Life,
> because we love our brothers—
> he who does not love dwells in death!
> Everyone who hates his brother is a murderer
> and you know that no murderer
> has Eternal Life dwelling in him.
> By this we have known Love:
> because he laid down his life for us,
> and we ought to lay down our lives for our brothers.
> Whoever has the world's means of life
> and sees that his brother has need
> and shuts his heart from him—
> how does the Love of God dwell in him?
> Little children, let us not love in word or in tongue
> but in work and in truth!   (I Jn. 3:13-18)

GUIDING SPIRIT

John 16

13   When She comes—the Spirit of Truth—
     She will guide you into all Truth,
     for She will not speak from Herself
     but will speak the things She hears
     and will proclaim to you what is coming.
14   She will glorify me
     for She will receive from me what is mine,
     therefore I said She receives from me what is mine
     and will proclaim it to you.

1   The Spirit of Truth guides us into the Whole Truth: Christ who is the Way, the Truth and the Life. Guided in the Spirit we enter into the Way who leads us into the inmost Life. In the Spirit we are able to recognize Christ, the True One.

The Spirit is given as our guide—not as one who *moves* us, but one who *shows* us the way. The Spirit is given *in our freedom*, respecting the fact that we must *move ourselves*, and so the Spirit is truly our Helper enabling us to see where we can move, but not in any sense dominating us. The Spirit shows us the Way, Christ, but we are the ones who respond, either by going with him in the Light and walking as he walks, or by turning from him and stumbling into the darkness.

The Spirit proclaims what is coming: Christ glorified. The Spirit is not given to us so that we can have knowledge of the future. Our lives and minds are always free. This freedom is at the heart of what it means to be human, and God's transforming Gift brings that freedom to perfection, in no way diminishing or destroying it. If we were to have (could have) knowledge of our future it could only be through a determination imposed upon us; otherwise in each present–moment of our growing lives we could *choose against* the "future" shown to us. We have often imagined what it might be like to live toward a "future" already known, and have easily seen the contradiction of our present experience—*we are truly free now* and so a human future takes shape from *our choices made now*. Within the bounds of our personal lives we create our future.

2   The Spirit receives from Christ everything he has received from the Father, and *This* is proclaimed. All the Father IS is Given in the Son and it is this *All* which the Spirit proclaims in Giving. The proclamation is not a message of words informing our minds. It is the inner opening of our consciousness so we ourselves can recognize Christ, and realize in our own direct experience of him that truly the Fullness is absolutely his and is becoming ours. This opening of consciousness occurs as we are guided in the Spirit *to come and see where Christ lives*: in–with–through all alive in Union with him. As we recognize Christ with his Glory now no longer hidden we realize we are beginning to see one another *transformed* with that Gift of Glory being unveiled:

> all of us with our faces unveiled
> as we reflect the Glory of the Lord
> are actually being transformed
> from Glory to Glory
> into that very reflection–image
> by the Lord, the Spirit.   (II Cor. 3:18)

LIFE–BEARING JOY

John 16

19   . . .
   In a little while you will not see me
   and in a little while longer you will see me.
20   Amen! Amen! I say to you:
   You will weep and wait while the world rejoices,
   you will suffer grief
   but your grief will change to joy.
21   When a woman gives birth she suffers
   because her hour has come,
   but when she brings forth the child
   she no longer remembers the pain
   in her joy that a man has been born into the world.
22   And so you indeed are now suffering,

but I will see you again
and your hearts will rejoice
and that joy no one shall take from you.

1   The Paschal Meal began the Last Day. The Twelve were gathered with
Jesus, receiving the Signs of Life in their Eating and Drinking. Whatever
their questions about the future, this present experience suggested the imminent triumph of the Anointed One who had come at last as Savior. But
their imagined worldly triumph would shortly prove to be nothing more
than a faint symbol of the reality. Before the day was over Death would
seem to be triumphant. Only after another day had passed in the suffering of loss would they awaken to what had actually happened. Then they
would realize: at the moment of dying Death had been destroyed as Life
had been Given.

The Paschal Meal had initiated the experience of the Signs of Life,
but the experience still awaited its completion. He was about to lay down
his life for his friends so that this final Love would generate his Life in them.
Then they would be able to recognize him alive in the Breaking of Bread.
This would be the experience of the Feast of the Lord in which they would
not merely receive the Signs of Life, but in him they themselves would
bring forth this Life under those Signs.

We experience God Given to us in Christ Life because we experience
God Giving Himself to us in the enlivening Spirit. In the Spirit—the Power
to live—we come alive within the Reality of God and so recognize Who
God now is to us: *Abba! Father!* The actuality of our experience of God
Giving is rooted in the fact that we experience we have the Power to give
What has been *Given* to us. Thus the image of childbirth is properly ours
as, One in Christ, we bear New Life into the human family: God *Giving*—
Spirit—Himself to us to be the Life *Given*—Son—so that we are One in
His Self-gift, and so that we in turn are those *Giving* God *Given* and others
are reborn, and still others through them.

2   The first disciples are the first parents in Christ, passing through their
pain of childbearing with him as he dies and they live, live to experience
the joy of recognizing him alive with them again in New Life. In the Feast
they take bread into their hands and say the words which proclaim their
new identity *he in them, they in him*: This is *my* body.

The suffering and joy of our first parents are uniquely theirs, never to be repeated. For them when Jesus died he seemed truly *gone* from their lives, *lost* in Death. They could not know that the very moment of dying was the wonder of rising—laying down life in love, transforming all into Life, the Gift-Love Who is God. Thus, their Easter joy was that of those who themselves were dead discovering they had Life. They arose in him. He saw them again, their hearts rejoiced with a joy which no one ever again could take from them—or from us. There is struggle in our being born anew and in our bearing Life for others, but it is not like that first struggle, for the Joy is already ours and we know it. Christ passed through death once for all and is alive, never again to die, and he is our Life never to be taken from us.

The Last Day has long been over. The New Day dawned and we live in that Light, learning to rejoice as we grow more and more in the *Love Given* in Christ and trusting our Power in the Spirit as we recognize ourselves to be those now *Giving Love*.

WITHIN CHRIST: WITHIN THE FATHER

John 16

25   I have been telling you these things in symbols,
       but the hour is coming
       when I will no longer speak to you in symbols,
       when I will make the Father known to you plainly.
26   On that day you will ask in my Name,
       and I do not say I shall ask the Father for you
27   for the Father Himself loves you
       because you have loved me
       and have believed I came forth from God.
28   I came forth from the Father
       and have come into the world,
       and now I leave the world
       and return to the Father.

1   Once again the Gospel community affirms their experience of revelation: it is in Christ, not in words—not even in his words. Hundreds upon

hundreds of times in his ministry among them he spoke to them of the Father, His Kingdom coming and the New Life about to be theirs. The hour of fulfillment is at hand when words give way to the reality they attempt to represent. This is not the promise of a distant future, it takes place in the Transformation which occurs that Last Day and dawns upon them with Easter.

Christ no longer speaks about his Father to us for the Father has been made known to us plainly: He is *our* Father and we know Him in our own experience—we are the ones who cry out our recognition *Abba! Father!* As we experience our reconstitution in Christ, he-and-we fully One, and truly sharing a single identity—the Only–Begotten of the Father—we ourselves recognize *our* Father. This is the completion of the earlier question of the core experience of Faith: *Have I been with you all this time, and still you have not known me? He who has seen me has seen the Father.* Have we been with Christ all this time—been alive in–through–with him, in Union, in ultimate identity—and still have not known ourselves?

2   Our experience should be most revealing to us at its concentrated center: when we pray. When all our inner consciousness is centered in the experience of God, we are aware that we seek to pray "with the mind of Christ". We address the words of prayer to our Father and confirm them invoking the Name of His Son. When we move into the depth of prayer, prayer too simple for words which give way to Spirit Silence, we can realize we are within the Name/Identity of Christ and so recognize our Father *from within*. No one seeks *for* us, and no seeking is needed for there is no distance separating, nothing to be bridged, no approach to be made to a Presence near or far.

From the beginning this is the immediate challenge in Christian experience: do we see ourselves praying *to* God as *to another*, or *within God* in Whom we truly live and Who fully lives in us? If we pray "through Christ our Lord" we can imagine *him* as *representing* us *to* God, but this is not the experience of the community of John: *I do not say I shall ask the Father for you, for the Father Himself loves you.* To pray *through* Christ—*in his Name*—is to pray through his identity which, as his Gift, is our identity. Only then can the words "our Father" cease to be mere words in a formula of prayer and become the moment of inmost Revelation *who we are.*

The Father Himself loves us for we have loved the Son and have believed. The word chosen to express the mode of love here is *phile* rather

than *agape*: love because we are already constituted in the bonds of relationship, as parent–with–child, brothers-and-sisters, or friends-together.
Our attention is not on the experience of Love as God's Self-gift but as
bonded sharing. As the Father loves the Son in that unitive Love, *phile*,
which we affirm in *begetting-and-begotten*, so the Father loves us. Because
we experience being loved as His Offspring, the Love that is *phile*, we can
recognize God *is* Love: *agape*, absolute Self-gift.

The Father loves us for we love the Son in the unitive Love—*phile*—
whereby he is the first-born of many brothers and sisters, but unitive Love
such that we many have become One in him. The Father loves One Only,
who is One All. Thus we believe *from our own experience* that he came
forth from God because we have received the Gift of Love—*agape*—and
live now in a Father's Love—*phile*.

Revelation is not truths but the One who is Truth. Words do not come
forth from God. Only the Person who is the Word comes. From within
the Reality of All God is he comes into complete human life, and all are
transformed to be able to return in him into the Glory which has become
ours.

ETERNAL LIFE: RECOGNIZE

John 17

1   Lifting his eyes toward heaven Jesus said—
Father, the hour has come!
Glorify Your Son
that Your Son may glorify You,
2   as You have given him Power over all flesh
that he might give Eternal Life
to all whom You have given him.
3   And this is Eternal Life:
that they know You the Only True God
and Jesus Christ whom You have sent.
4   I have glorified You on earth
completing the Work You gave me to do.
5   And now, Father, glorify me with Yourself
with the Glory I had with You
before the world existed.

1   The great prayer of Glory marks the end of the Paschal Meal and the beginning of the Feast of the Lord. In its words the Gospel community gives expression to the Revelation we experience in Christ.

The first word is *Father*. As spoken by Jesus it is *Abba*, the warm and joyous recognition by a little child of a loving Father. Abba is the expression of trust and delight in one known only as the living source of a child's love, a love still too innocent to be aware of the possibility of awe, much less of fear. *When you pray say: Abba*... To have learned to say Abba as our first word of Faith is to have recognized *Person* as the center of our Faith experience, rather than things–ideas–truths. In the complete Person of Christ to discover our full personhood born anew is to awaken to the joyous recognition of Who God really is in our lives—*Abba!* As *these* little children we are uninterested in an Almighty God, an All–knowing God, an Infinite, a King or a Judge—God conceived by the mind seeking to grasp Him from the "outside". We now know Him *from within*: He is our Joy.

2   The prayer of Glory flows from the loving first word. As the Father manifests the Glory of the Son, the Son shows what the Glory of the Father actually is: Life–giving. The Father has given the Son Power over all living things so that he can give God's own Life to all. This is how we know Christ to be Son in Glory, for we have experienced our Transformation from life to Life. We know we are now alive within the Living God, because we recognize Him to be truly Abba. And so the Son is glorified and glorifies the Father. We are glorified and glorify our Father.

It is in this that we realize we have been reborn and now live the Eternal Life: we ourselves experience the Father and know He alone is the True One, as we know the Son sent to us. The Only True One is the One we experience as truly *our Abba*. Anything else is an *image* of God, and any image is not itself the Reality. God known through idea and concept is not *God Himself*. The True God *truly known* must be personally encountered, not through the medium of thought seeking to represent God.

3   The Power of Christ is not a form of knowledge enlightening our minds so that we can grasp a revelation—it is the Power to live: to live unitively, he–we together, sharing a single ultimate Identity, and as One Person experiencing God, within God, as God. The Father is glorified on earth as the Son completes the Work: Life–giving. The Work of Christ in him and in us is not a task to be done, an accomplishment; it is that *we may live*

and live fully—it is that *we may* BE *as God* IS. Only in this can God really be glorified, as His Glory is His inmost Power, the Power to be the Living God, the Power of Eternal Life. If His Life is Given to be shared, then He is glorified. His Glory is made manifest *in us* as It is, not through (ultimately falsifying) images manifested *to us* as It is not!

Father, glorify me with Yourself. . .There is no other Glory. This is the Glory of the Son from the beginning, truly Son of God truly his Father. The Son coming forth from the Father into human life comes as one of us, and we are not ourselves glorious. The Son grows into human life as Jesus grows to his full stature. In his final moment as he lays down life he gives All he is, and we receive All he is. And then we know: his is the Glory from the beginning, the Glory Who is God.

The prayer of Glory, thus, is the prayer of fulfillment. Jesus, grown to Fullness in his Anointing, is fully within the Father. He has grown in his human life to Fullness by loving his own to the end, completely, laying down life in Love. As we are loved with that Love, we are drawn into complete Union, and he–we become One. Reborn, we grow in our personal lives to our full stature in Christ, to be fully within the Father. Only God is glorious. Abba, glorify us with Yourself!

UNITIVE CHRIST

John 17

6   I have manifested Your Name
      to the men You gave me from the world.
      They were Yours
      and You gave them to me
      and they have kept Your Word.
7   Now they realize
      all You have given me
      are indeed from You.
8   For I have given them
      the words you gave me
      and they have received them
      and so really know I came forth from You,
      and have believed You sent me.

9   I am asking this for them—
I ask nothing for the world
but only for those You have given me
because they are Yours:
10   and all mine are Yours
and Yours mine,
and I have been glorified in them—
11   I am no longer in the world
but they are in the world
and I am coming to You.
Holy Father
firmly keep in Your Name
those you have given me
that they may be One as We are!

1   Christ has manifested the Name of God—the inmost Self God actually is. It is not a name merely spoken, nor even a sacred name revered in ritual silence. And it is not a further or even a final truth about God. It is God Himself made manifest in the living Christ. It is the Father now *Given in* the Son to those the Father has *Given to* the Son, to be *his*. The Hidden Mystery of God is now opened to be entered, and so known from within.

As we receive and keep the True Word of God—Christ—we can realize at last that the *all* the Son receives from the Father includes *us*. We are awakened by the words of Christ (as he speaks, acts and lives in our midst) to recognize him: we ourselves really know and so believe he comes forth from the Father sent into our lives.

2   *All mine are Yours and Yours mine.* The Son is glorified in the living Power of the Father, his from the beginning. And he is glorified in that *Power Given*, which now becomes ours. The Name is manifested as we are transformed, coming alive in Christ Life, reborn through the Giving of the Spirit and becoming One with the Given Son. We are the *"Yours–and–mine"* of his Glory: the Power of Life Which alone is glorious and those brought to Life who are thus made glorious. In his prayer of Glory Christ asks for one thing only for those alive in him, that we might be kept firmly in the Name so that we can be One in the Only Oneness of Father and Son. We live transformed in a world still to be transformed: we have been

Given Life so that we can become those Giving Life. We must be kept in that Life, for our identity is no longer with a world untransformed but with the Firstborn who, beginning with us, is making all things new.

Christ seeks nothing for the world—nothing but *people* who are in the world and in him, who are his first–fruits and who can thus bear fruit that will last. To be kept firmly in the Name, to be One as Father and Son are, is *to be Given to be Giving.* It is to be the Power of Life in its *seed*—which is fruitless if it remains alone (Jn. 12:24), but which is fully alive only after dying as it brings forth new life in its self–multiplication.

> A sower went out to sow his seed . . .
> and some fell into good soil
> and when grown it produced fruit a hundredfold.   (Lk. 8:5, 8)

HOLINESS IN THE TRUTH

John 17

13   But now I come to You,
       and I say all this while in the world
       that they may have my joy
       wholly fulfilled in themselves.
14   I have given them Your Word
       and the world has hated them
       since they are not of the world
       just as I am not of the world.
15   I do not ask You
       to take them out of the world
       but to keep them from evil.
16   They are not of the world
       just as I am not of the world.
17   Make them Holy in the Truth—
       Your Word is Truth!
18   As You have sent me into the world
       I have also sent them into the world
19   and for their sake I make myself Holy
       that they also may be made Holy in Truth.

1   Three times the gift of joy is promised to the disciples. To dwell in Love is to receive the joy of Christ and it is made full (15:11). The suffering of giving birth to the New Life, already beginning, will shortly be changed to the joy no one can ever take away (16:22). Now he is about to go into death, laying down his life in Love so they can be reborn in Life. His joy is to be completely fulfilled in them immediately in their own unfolding lives, and not merely at some distant moment of culmination. They/we are already transformed in Christ and so his full joy is already reality. But, consequently, the joy is experienced in the midst of what seems to be the contradiction of Christ Life: the Gift can be rejected, Love can be hated—yet, even confronting death, there is the inmost Joy in the newborn's cry *Abba!* He returns within the Father *with us* and we are with him where he truly is: *with us*. And we remain in the untransformed world seeking to bring all to Transformation as we minister, serving God to people.

> . . . As ministers of God . . .
> in the Word of Truth,
> in the Power of God . . .
> as afflicted but always rejoicing,
> as poor but enriching many,
> as having nothing but possessing All.   (II Cor. 6:4,10)

2   To make us *Holy in the Truth* is to fulfill the command which stands at the center of all the precepts of the Torah. To fulfill this command implies the fulfillment of all the others:

> You must not profane My Holy Name
> so that I may be proclaimed Holy
> among the sons of Israel,
> I YHWH Who make you holy.   (Lev. 22:32)

To proclaim Holy the Name—*Kiddush Ha-Shem*—is to live always observing the commands of the Torah. Living out the precepts is to live a perfect human life, perfect because the God–given plan for life, the Torah, is perfect. *Kiddush Ha-Shem* is fulfilled each time a choice is confronted and one chooses that which would proclaim the Holiness of God—rejecting that which would profane/dishonor Him. The things one does become manifestations of the Hiddenness of God: the awesome Sacredness is reflected in human actions which do not dare to violate His Will—the fear of the Lord which is seen as the beginning of wisdom (Ps. 111:10).

> Behold: this day I set before you
> life and prosperity
> or death and disaster. . .   (Deut. 30:15)
> . . .the Torah which endures forever—
> those who keep her live,
> those who desert her die!   (Bar. 4:1)

In the Eucharistic discourse of John 6, Jesus identifies himself, the Word of Truth come forth from the Father, as the bread of God come to give Life to the world (v.33). It is the Father's Will to give Eternal Life to all who see the Son and believe in him (v.40).

> It has been written in the prophets
> *And they shall all be taught by God.*
> Anyone who hears and learns from the Father
> comes to me.   (Jn. 6:45)

To proclaim Holy the Name of God is not to live a perfect human life according to the plan of the Torah, but to be taught by God, to hear the Word of Truth, to see the Son, to come to him and so to receive Eternal Life. In laying down his life for us Christ manifests the full Holiness of God—not the awesome Holiness of a God to be feared, but the absolute Holiness of Love. For our sakes Christ makes himself Holy—reveals the Reality of Love by living It: living, dying, rising. And thus we are made Holy in the Truth, Holy in Christ as he is Holy.

The inner Mystery of what it means to proclaim the Holiness of God is not manifested in *what we do* but in *who we are*. We are persons alive in Christ, the Eternal Life of the Father Given to all who see and believe. It is because we are *these persons* that What we do can bear testimony to the Truth.

What must we do if we are to do the works of God? (v.28) is a question about *things*: what commands of the Torah proclaim God's Holiness? Jesus gave them this answer:

> This is the work of God:
> believe in the One He has sent. (v.29)

REVELATION IN UNION

John 17

20 Not only do I ask this for them
    but also for those who through their word
    will believe in me—
21 That all may be One
    as You, Father, in me
    and I in You,
    may they thus be in Us
    so that the world may believe
    You did send me.
22 And I have given them
    the Glory You gave me
    so that they may be One
    just as We are One:
23 I in them
    and You in me,
    may they be so completely One
    that the world will realize
    You have sent me
    and have loved them
    as You have loved me.

1   As the Discourse draws to its close the meaning of the Paschal Mystery
proclaimed at the beginning of the Meal—return to the Father in the complete love of all who are His—is made clear in a great two–fold prayer of
Union. Twice before Jesus speaks of the Life of Union now opening for
his disciples.

> . . .where I am you also shall be. . .
> On that day you will realize:
> I in my Father,
> and you in me,
> and I in you!. . .
> If anyone loves me
> he will keep my word

and my Father will love him
and We will come to him
and make Our home with him.   (14:3,20,23)

This first promise of Union is made through the image of the dwelling-place, the House of God. The disciples shall dwell with the Lord forever but not in a Temple—they themselves are to become the home of God. Then later he speaks of the imminent fulfillment of the promise because they have received him, the Living Message:

Now they realize
all You have given me
are indeed from You.
For I have given them
the words You gave me
and they have received them
and so really know I came forth from You,
and have believed You sent me.   (17:7–8)

But now the prayer–promise of Union reaches out to all through the ministry of Life: begun by Jesus in his first disciples, then, as they become One in him, he–they extend this Union through living witness—through their words which shout out the Good News more and more and more can come to believe. It is Union open without limit, embracing all given the Son by the Father. And the prayer of Union insists there is only One Union: the Oneness that is Father–and–Son is itself the Oneness of Son–and–all. The Divine–human unity of Incarnation is unique—It alone can encompass all, beginning in Christ and ceaselessly extending to draw in all.

2   The basis of our Oneness is asserted to be nothing other than the inherent Oneness within God: *One as You, Father, in me and I in You.* Because of this unity it will be possible for still others to come to believe that the Father sent the Son. This cannot be anything other than the Union of Incarnation. How did the first disciples come to believe? Because they themselves encountered, came to know and love, person–with–person, the man Jesus, and then through the Spirit to recognize he is the total human embodiment of All God is.

Through the *Giving* that is the Spirit their inward eyes were opened and they saw God *Given* in Christ. *He who sees me sees the Father.* The Giving of the Spirit begins in the moment of loving, the moment one responds to another unitively as person. There are natural moments of response, beginning with the infant's *smile of recognition* on seeing the mother's face having grown into the experience of being loved. And there is the Divine moment of response:

> In this is Love:
> not that we have loved God
> but that He has loved us . . .
> We are to love, then,
> because He first loved us.   (I Jn. 4:10,19)

As with the first disciples, the world of people through time will be able to come to believe God Given if they see Him as He is: Incarnate. They will see Him as He is Incarnate *now*—the True Image embodied uniquely in the human–Divine reality of Jesus Christ himself, as he limitlessly extends the unique Incarnation he is by making us truly One with him. People can see Christ as he fully is, in–through–with all who are his. There are not many Incarnations, not many True Images. There is but One: Christ is All and in all (Col. 3:11).

3   We are truly One with God in Christ because we have been given the Glory of God which is Christ's. In coming into human life the Glory of Christ was veiled until that moment in the Spirit when he can be seen as he fully is. In the Resurrection the disciples recognize him alive–in–Glory, human and Divine, *My Lord and my God* (Jn. 20:28). The Glory that is his with the Father from the beginning is restored to our sight. And it is ours as we are One with him.

For ancient Israel the Glory of the Lord, the *Kabod*, was the unique manifestation of the Presence in Power of the Only One. The inner Power of God to be God, the Hidden Mystery He IS, became visible to people through the effects of His Power. As human beings and the human world responded to God, whether faithfully or rebelliously, God's Presence was revealed in the acts which flowed from His Power. All reflected the Glory of God. In the image of the cloud of blinding light, the *Shekinah*, the Torah celebrates the times when the Presence in Power assumed an almost tangible manifestation of Glory—the *Shekinah* atop Mount Sinai, coming into the

Sanctuary Tent of the desert, and as the terrifying sign of judgment up-
holding Moses before faithless people.

The *Kabod* of the Lord was His and His alone. To propose that a human
being could possess this Glory was a blasphemy, in making someone the
equal of the Only God besides Whom there could be no other. It was the
abomination of an idol. It was for this that Jesus was condemned when
he asserted before the Sanhedrin—

> . . .you will see the Son of Man
> seated at the right hand of Power,
> coming on the clouds of heaven.
>   (Mk. 14:62; Mt. 26:64; Lk. 22:69)

But those who condemned him had not recognized in him the fact
of the Glory. He was no idol, but the embodiment of the Presence in Power.
He had not usurped Glory, it was his with the Father before the world existed. In the tragedy of rejection they had failed to see. As Paul says,

> we speak the Wisdom of God in Mystery. . .
> if they had known
> they would not have crucified
> the Lord of Glory.   (I Cor. 2:7–8)

We have been given the Glory of Christ, and this also is no usurpa-
tion. We are not "other gods". There are not many glories. There is only
One real manifestation of the One God: Christ the True One who shares
All God is. And he shares this All with us by opening his Union to us.
Christ gives us the Glory of God, the inmost Power whereby God IS God,
the Power of Selfhood. It is in this Gift alone that we can really be One
just as he and the Father are One. And our Union is asserted to be nothing
less than that. He does not pray that we be one *something like* his and the
Father's Oneness, but *may they be One just as We are One*. We are not to
be given a glory which merely reflects Divine Glory, but the Glory of the
Self of God.

4   The prayer of Union is two-fold. One of the characteristics of Johannine composition (one reminiscent of the pattern of "doublets" throughout
the Hebrew Scriptures) is the use of various forms of repetition to ensure

that we take at full value what is being emphasized. The force of such repetition is the insistence on the literal meaning of what is expressed. Thus,

> Think of the Love the Father has given us,
> that we may be called the children of God—
> and we are!—   (I Jn. 3:1)

And here in the conclusion of the great prayer of Union we find perhaps the most important instance of a repetition demanding the literal meaning.

> *I in them*
> *and You in me,*
> *may they be so completely One*
> *that the world will realize*
> *You have sent me...*

As we are to be One *just as* Father and Son are One, so we are to be *completely One*. And once again, it is in this that it will be possible for people to realize the Father sends the Son. For they can see him as he really is: he–we completely One. The reality of Christ is not to be grasped by trusting the testimony of others that *they* have beheld him and so *we* should believe them. Rather, Christ can be met and recognized directly by encountering him–us in his–our continuing Christ Life.

It is quite clear from the careful repetition that our unity is not a merely human social effect derived as an image of the inner Union of God in Christ. The world is not to be drawn to realize the reality of Christ by being impressed that his disciples lead a loving, caring, unitive life together as a human imitation of Christ. (The disciples of many masters live in such a way as to impress us with the sincerity and beauty of lives enriched by their great teachers. And in a metaphorical sense we can "see" the master in such faithful disciples. But the master is not really alive in them.)

The heart of the Christian experience is life unified person–with–person so completely One that there is only One Life in the full Union of the many persons.

> *To see me is to see the Father...*
> To see me as I fully am:
> *I in them, You in me...*
> To see Us is to see...

5   As the first statement of Union identifies the basis of our being One—
the Glory given us—so the second affirms as ours the Love which is the
inner Union of Father and Son. Glory is the manifestation of the Power,
the Selfhood of God. And that Power is recognized in Christ as the Power
to give, give absolutely. Throughout the Torah and the Prophets the Power
of God is thought of as Might: mighty acts in the convulsions of nature
as flood and earthquake, fire and storm; mighty acts in the rule over peoples
as the triumph of armies, vengeance upon the wicked, liberation of the
oppressed. In Christ the Power of God is finally revealed as it is: Love, *Given*
once–for–all in the Son and always *Giving* through the Spirit.

We are One because we ourselves have God's Glory, the manifestation of His Presence in Power—because we have that Power in Christ for
our own, the Love God is.

And the world will be able to realize the Father did send His Son and
does love Us as He eternally loves him.

> your life has been hidden with Christ in God;
> whenever Christ appears—he is our Life—
> then you shall appear with him in Glory.   (Col. 3:3–4)

GLORY OF LOVE

John 17

24   Father, I wish that those You have given me
    may be with me where I am,
    that they may see my Glory You gave me
    because You have loved me
    before the foundation of the world.

25   Just Father,
    the world has not known You
    but I have known You,
    and these have known You have sent me.

26   And I have made known Your Name to them
    and will continue to make It known,
    that the Love with which You loved me
    may be in them
    and I in them.

1   Our Union in Christ is a reality here–and–now. It is not a promise for the future, but a promise fulfilled. Yet the fulfilled promise has an on-going future. All of us receive the Gift of Christ Life into ongoing personal lives. This is true of each and is equally true of the ongoing interpersonal life of the whole community gathered into Oneness in Christ over space and time.

To be with Christ where he is, is to be with him as he lives here with us. It is here that we see his Glory—begin to see the Glory that becomes more and more dazzling the more we look upon it.

But Glory is not an *it*, a *thing*—the Glory is Love, the Self–gift of God to persons. The more we *see and recognize* the persons of our lives as those to whom God is *Given* and *Giving*, the more we behold Christ in Glory. But we must see and recognize all these persons, for Christ gives God to all, to those who seem to reject as well as to those who seem to receive. The wonder is not that we love God, but that He loves us first.

Christ loves all, completely, to the end. He, the Lord and Master, serves God to us all as all are called into the Great Supper, the Feast of the Lord.

2   To see and recognize Christ in Glory, to dwell within him in Union, is a Gift already present which we make more and more our own as we live the Christ Life. But this Gift is not a reward. The Self–gift of God is ours, consciously ours, so that we in turn can minister to others. The open-ing scene of the Supper teaches us the meaning of Christ serving. The final prayer of Union speaks of our Oneness in Christ as that same serv-ing. Being One, recognizing him in Glory by being loved and so loving in response—this and this alone will enable still others to believe and realize God's Self–gift for themselves.

I have come
that they may have life
and have it to the full.   (Jn. 10:10)

Christ comes within us always for that one purpose: to be the Living God *Given* in our open *Giving* of the One we have received.

I have made Your Name known
His Name: the Only True One
and continue to make It known

in the ceaseless Giving of the True Gift—
that Love may be in them
that I may be in them.

three _____

FAITH:
THE REALITY OF CHRIST

THE ONLY–BEGOTTEN WORD

John 1

1 In the beginning was the Word
and the Word was with God
and the Word was God.
2 He was with God in the beginning.
3 Through him all things came to be
and without him not one thing came to be.

4 In him was Life
and the Life was the Light of people,
5 and the Light shines in the darkness
and the darkness did not overpower it.
. . .

9   This was the True Light
which enlightens everyone
coming into the world.

10 He was in the world,
and the world had come to be through him,
and the world did not know him!

11 He came to his own home,
and his own people did not receive him!

12 But to all who did receive him
he gave the Power to become Offspring of God,
to all who believe in his Name—

13 those born not of blood–descent,
nor of the urge of flesh,
nor of the will of man,
but of God!

14 And the Word became flesh
and raised his Sanctuary–Tent among us
and we beheld his Glory:
the Glory of the Only–Begotten of the Father
full of Gift and Truth!

    . . .

16 We have all received from his Fullness,
Gift upon Gift:

    . . .

18 No one has ever seen God—
the Only–Begotten God,
Who dwells within the embrace of the Father,
makes Him known.

1   The Johannine Gospel as we now have it represents the unification of several previously independent texts into a single document. Thus, the Last Supper Discourse draws together at least three separate Discourse texts, and the present Chapter 21 was originally a completely self–contained "Gospel of the Resurrection Faith". What we now speak of as the Johannine Gospel Prologue (Chapter 1, vv.1–18) was originally the great Hymn of Faith, an experiential creed, of the Johannine community.

    When incorporated as the introduction to the full Gospel sometime before the end of the first century, editorial additions were made reflecting theological disputes (with surviving sectaries of John the Baptist: vv.6-7, 15) and the tragic break with continuing Judaism (v.17). In removing these editorial additions we discover an amazing and unique characteristic of this creed, setting it apart from the other New Testament creeds: it is universalistic and transhistorical. There is no mention of Jesus Christ by name, no reference to his suffering, death and resurrection as such. There is no explicit connection made between the tradition of Israel and the new experience of this Faith–community. In all probability this intended universalism reflected the origins of the Johannine Gathering—from among Greeks, Hellenized Syrians and Samaritans, rather than from Diaspora Jewry. In our own era of open–ended ecumenism this universalism takes on a new and unforeseen dimension: the core of the Christian experience can be expressed authentically in ways totally free from the particularism (and hence an always implied separatism) of history—either earth–history or the inevitably independent other–planet–histories of our multi–world cosmos. The essentially historical nature of Christianity—the actual human being Jesus of Nazareth, self–giving at a real time and place, to people, all people, all of whom are personally real—is insisted upon in *our historical moments* of Faith–experience (as in receiving him, vv.12 ff., and known–by–embrace, v.18). But the ultimate Truth of Faith is celebrated transhistorically for all times, places, peoples and persons.

2   *In the beginning. . . the Word was God.* The great Johannine Hymn of Faith opens a new Genesis—

In the beginning. . .the Spirit of God. . .(Gen. 1:1-2). The ancient vision of creation stands at the threshold of all that comes to be: in the symbol of Divine Breath (*Ruah*, "Spirit", the "Living Self" of God) hovering like a life–giving bird above her nest of fledglings. This is the beginning-point, the lifeless void breathed into by the Source of Life. It is a vision which necessarily must begin *outside* the always–Hidden God. The vision begins with what we can see—our world, ourselves—looking back to the furthest edge of our limits and realizing the significance of those limits: we are not our own source, there is Another.

The new Johannine vision of creation begins *before* creation, and *within* the God now revealed in Christ. God has *breathed* His Living Self into us, and through this Spirit we are reborn in the Son and so *within him* come alive within the Father. And we begin to come to a new consciousness *within* the Reality of God—a new Mind in Christ. And we begin to recognize.

The ancients thought of their growth in awareness of themselves in God as a growth in Wisdom through words. They recognized Truth in words felt powerfully in the Spirit, words so enlivening as to be Words coming with the Breathing of God. For the prophets, these were the Messages of God, the Word of the Lord. For the Tradition of Israel these Messages are the Word of the Lord in the Scriptures.

3   For those reborn into Christ there is a new awareness: Christ himself is the one–and–only Message of God—the Good News: *All God is and all we are have become One.* Christ, and Christ alone, is the Word of God.

> You search the Scriptures
> because you think that in them
> you have Eternal Life!
> But they themselves bear witness to me,
> and yet you refuse to come to me
> to have Life!   (Jn. 5:39)

Christ himself—*not Scriptures*—is the Life.

The Word of God is not a message of words. Words can do no more than bear witness in our minds to what we experience in our consciousness. In Christ we do not experience merely our own truths *about* God: we begin to experience God as God is, the True One Himself incarnate in the Only True Image. And we experience by recognizing the Person of Christ, recognizing by the personal response of love. And we realize that *to know by love* is to know with a "knowledge" beyond knowledge (Eph. 3:12). In Christ we can finally come to realize that God does not send us *things*—words, messages, truths—He sends Himself in His True Image, the Image who does not *represent* God but who *presents* God. All other words can do no more than bear witness to the Life, they cannot be that Life. They are only *words about the Word of God.*

4   In the ancient Genesis God commands *Let there be light* (1:3) and the shaping of the universe begins, with the dividing of light from dark. In the new creation all reality exists within the Word within God. All come forth through the Image, becoming individuals and so one by one dividing, each itself distinct and thus unique. For, paradoxically, each individual precisely as *divided from others* points back to the Undivided God. The fragment proclaims Wholeness.

For we know only in fragments
and we prophesy only in fragments
but when That which is Whole comes
then that made of fragment passes away. . .
Now I know only a fragment
but then I shall fully know
just as I am fully known!   (I Cor. 13:9,10,12)

For the ancient Genesis light was a dazzling first *thing* of creation. For the Johannine creation all such *things* arising into existence through the Word fail to hold our attention because we have caught sight of the Word himself in the Light which is Life. He is *Light for people*. This is not the light/energy that explodes through a void filling it with a universe. He is the Light–Life Given within us, filling us so that we cannot be void. What would be darkness if we were no more than *things* is transformed into Light as we, *living persons*, receive *him* to be our Life—person–with–person.

He alone is the True Light, as he alone is the Word. God Self–given in Christ is not a message of words to enlighten our minds. We receive the Self of God, nothing else and nothing less. God does not *have things*; if He gives, all He can give is Himself. God is not divided—He is One, Whole; if He gives, He must give All He Himself is. Christ is not a light illuminating our minds so that we can know something about God.

The God Who said:
Let light shine out of darkness—
is He Who has shone in our hearts
to be the radiance of our consciousness
of the Glory of God on the Face of Christ.   (2 Cor. 4:6)

5   The vision of creation and re–creation in Christ must always include the Mystery of rejection–yet–glorification at the center. This Hymn of Faith not only proclaims a celebration of Christ Life, it also proclaims sacrifice. The One Source of all comes into their midst and the countless many do not recognize.

Left to ourselves we are so caught up in our divided individualities—each struggling to assert *me!*, struggling against all others—that we can fail to recognize one who embodies the undivided Whole. Even though we do have the urge to reach out to others, the very success in touching person and being touched as person and thus forming *us* always seems to suggest *us and not–them!*

The one who comes in the Name of the Lord to bring Blessing is a Gift indeed, but to receive we must change—change from the narrowness of self–assertion that desperately fears the loss of our secure little limits. We think we must possess things–for–ourselves or we will be lost. We know that everyone needs things to exist—not to need any longer suggests not to exist any longer. We can fail to recognize the Gift, God Himself, to be our Life—the One Who alone does not *need* and Who absolutely *is.* We can cling to a narrow self and reject because we see nothing but ourselves. We can all too easily insist that our little needy selves must be preserved, rejecting anything and anyone else. Our image of who we think we are becomes a "god" who must be served.

> But if indeed our Good News has been veiled
> it has been veiled from those who are perishing.
> The "god" of this age
> has blinded the thought
> of those who disbelieve
> so there will not shine forth
> the enlightenment of the Good News
> of the Glory of Christ
> who is the Image of God.   (2 Cor. 4:3-4)

As long as we cling to our divided selves we are perishing. When we turn from the false image to the True Image and begin to see and receive, we begin to change

> If indeed you heard him
> and were taught by him
> as the Truth is in Jesus. . .
> you must be made new
> in your conscious self*
> and put on the new person
> created corresponding to God,
> in uprightness and holiness of Truth.   (Eph. 4:21, 23, 24)

6   To receive the Self–gift of God in Christ is to enter the new creation.

*Literally: *in the spirit of your mind*

The Divine Power of Life is *Given* and in him we become a new creature, the Offspring of God. All who come to *know–by–loving* the real Christ come alive in him—reconceived and reborn so that together he–we are truly One and so as the One Only embody All God is. He, the Only–Begotten, shares himself with us. There are not many offspring of God—Christ and all who are drawn into Union with him are inseparably One, person–with–person

> . . .we all attain the unity of Faith
> and the full awareness of the Son of God—
> until we are a completely mature Man
> as measured by the stature
> of the Fullness of Christ.   (Eph. 4:13)

Our rebirth does not have its source in us. It is Gift. The transformation in which we grow into the Self Given in Christ is not merely a further natural development of human persons. It is not a process of perfecting the limited human self. As a human being embodying the Fullness of God, Jesus Christ's human reality and Divine Reality are in a Union so complete that he is not two beings. And so we assert his unique Source: Life begotten within God and born into human life through a woman. Our Union centered through him is so complete that we, who are born into human life through women, realize that Source is his–ours. We share his Reality *Begotten–of–God* and so are reborn into Life through the Spirit.

7   The Johannine community's Hymn of Faith expresses a movement in experience: from the vision of creation coming forth from within God–the–Word to the Divine Reality of the Light of Life within human life; from the Mystery of rejection or acceptance to the Power of transformation, the Only–Begotten begetting. Finally there is the celebration of Glory, as the *God–with–us* is fully revealed.

The Word of God, within God and through Whom all have come forth, Himself comes forth within creation. Two of the most ancient of Israel's symbols proclaim it: the Sanctuary and Glory. The Word became *flesh*— God actually *embodied* as human. And this human embodiment is now the Temple of God's Presence in Power.

The verbal expression is simplicity itself, a single Greek word *he–raised–a–tent*, and all the experience of the Mosaic Sanctuary–Tent of the wilderness is both evoked and changed. The Sanctuary (and later the Temple in Jerusalem) was to be the one place on earth where God's Presence in

Power would dwell so that we could approach. But the Sanctuary was always a paradoxical sign: the Immanence of God present almost tangibly in the Holy of Holies, but also the Transcendence of God cut off within the Holy of Holies, since only the High Priest could enter once each year on the Day of Atonement with the blood of the sacrifice for sin. The God of the ancient Sanctuary was present, dwelling as in a House, but unapproachable; present but awesome. The sign of His Presence was the blinding light–cloud manifesting the unique Glory of God. Much of the religious consciousness of Israel was shaped by traditions of the *Shekinah*, God manifesting His Glory.

> Moses said: I beg You, show me Your Glory. And He said: I will cause My Splendour to pass in front of you, and will pronounce before you My Name YHWH. I have compassion on whom I will, and show mercy to whom I will. But (He said) you cannot look at My Face, for man cannot see Me and live! And YHWH said: Here is a place for you to stand by Me on the rock, and while My Glory passes by I will put you in a cleft in the rock and cover you with My Hand as I pass by. Then I will take my Hand away and you shall see My Back, but My Face shall not be seen.   (Exod. 33:18-23)

It is a primitive but vivid image of God present but overpoweringly so, and thus to be feared. This image of Splendour is the traditional sign of the Sanctuary-Tent and then of the Temple, as at their dedications the *Shekinah* is seen descending upon and entering the Holy of Holies. For the first Christians the *Shekinah* is this same sign of Presence, but now within the human reality of Christ, the new and everlasting Sanctuary in whom God dwells with us. This is the Gospel image of the Transfiguration on the mount: the disciples fail to realize that his splendour is not that of a prophet—a mere reflection of the Divine Splendour—until the Cloud overshadows them and the Voice proclaims him His Son.

But there is a more important change. This Sanctuary with its Glory is not a place of awe in our midst, causing us to keep back in fear. He is one of us, welcoming us, drawing us to himself so that we can enter within and see the Glory face-to-face. In Christ *everyone can see Me and Live!* In fact, only if we come to recognize the Only True God and the One He has sent can we have Eternal Life.

> The hour is coming
> when neither on this mountain
> nor in Jerusalem
> will you worship the Father. . .
> The hour is coming—
> in fact it is now!—
> when true worshippers
> will worship the Father
> in Spirit and Truth
> for the Father seeks such
> to worship Him.
> God is Spirit
> and those who worship
> must worship in Spirit and Truth.   (Jn. 4:21, 23–24)

We worship in Spirit and Truth as we recognize and respond to the Gift: God—Spirit—eternally *Giving* His Self to us to be our own, in the eternally *Given*—the Truth, the True Image, the Only-Begotten, Christ. It is not a Torah we receive, a new Law to be the pattern of an ideal humanity perfecting natural life. Such was the ancient gift made through Moses, a gift for a life of uprightness and holy justice, the response of loving obedience to a merciful God. We receive Gift upon Gift: life transformed into Life, countless human persons in the Union of Christ. We receive from the Fullness of God: into our own reborn selves we receive the Self-Gift of the Whole God to be our Power of New Life.

8   There is grandeur in the sweep of this Johannine proclamation of Faith:

> the eternal God in the Word
> the creation
> Life coming into life
> the crisis of rejection
> the re-creation as Divine Offspring
> the living Sanctuary
> the Gift of Glory.

Finally, there is the vision of God, seen face-to-face. And it is in this final expression that the Gospel community unveils the true depth of their Faith experience. For here grandeur gives way to absolute simplicity.

Of all the levels of experience in the human person which could be our opening of consciousness into God, it is the experience of infancy which proclaims the Christ vision. It is not a sentimentality about infancy, but the fact of our own no–longer–remembered beginnings of the awakening of ourselves as persons. As we have developed our insight into the formation and growth of active personhood, we more and more realize the life–forming power of the simple act of *holding* a child. The way we hold—touch, hug, embrace—communicates *who we are* to the infant and there is an immediate matching response. If the holding is secure, warm, affectionate, relaxed, loving, we unveil to the child's consciousness we are *that* person, and as in a mirror the new person of the child begins to become such a person in response. Love responds to love. It is the true image of another experienced directly by an intimate sharing of life, through a depth communication body to body, rather than through mere words mind to mind.

This fundamental human experience becomes the way to express what it really means to say *God has revealed Himself, we have seen God*. It is not mere words, not mere sights. Because God loves, gives Himself, shares All He is, this is the True Image found in Christ, and the human person–reality reflects the True One in response. The simple human image *a father embracing-hugging his child in love and the child lovingly hugging back* becomes the clearest expression of the Word within God: *loved, loving.* It is the image of consciousness deeper than mind, a consciousness that is the dynamic power of life of a person.

It is this experience which alone truly reveals God. The Only–Begotten who lives in the embrace of the Father (lit: *upon His bosom*) makes God known. We are not told about God. We ourselves, now in Union with the Son, begin to "feel that embrace"—we begin to feel our own responding as we begin to change, to become persons who more and more reflect the One Who gives His Self. We begin to see, to recognize, as we recognize the persons we are becoming in Gift.

Throughout his ministry of all the words Jesus could have used to express his relationship in God, he chose *Abba*, the word of warmth and love shouted out by small children in delight as they hugged their fathers. He always—and only—prayed "Abba. . ." In the Scriptures and traditions of Israel there were great words of power and awe. But Jesus spoke the word of the smallest children, a word which remained in the experience of the eldest of his hearers as the joyous recognition of the *person of love*. This is the way to express the ultimate meaning of the *vision of God in Christ*: we *see* because we *are embraced* and we *respond, becoming* the One we see.

CREATION AND RE–CREATION: IMAGE AND GATHERING

Colossians 1

15   He is the Image of the Invisible God,

First–born before all creation
16   because in him all things were created
in the heavens and on earth,
the visible and the invisible,
whether thrones or lordships
or rulers or authorities—
17   all have been created through him and for him.
And he exists before all things
and all are sustained in him.

18   And he is the Head of the Body, the Gathering.

He is the beginning, First–born from the dead
so that in everything he should be first,
19   because All the Fullness was pleased to dwell in him
20   and through him to reconcile all to Himself
making peace through the Blood of his Cross—
everything through him,
whether on the earth or in the heavens.

1   The great experiential creed of Colossians witnesses to the Pauline teaching of the Good News in both words and phrases characteristically emphasized by Paul, but, even more importantly, in the centrality of the Christ Paul himself knew: the Christ of Resurrection. Unlike the later Patristic creeds, those of the earliest Gathering directly reflect the Faith experience of the Believers, rather than philosophical concepts seeking to express intellectual understanding. Also, the earliest creeds are nor formulated around elements of the four Gospel accounts (born of the Virgin,

suffering under Pontius Pilate, buried, risen on the third day, ascending to come again). It is the here–and–now Christ of Union who is the significance of the Faith of the living people as they give voice to their actual experience.

The Colossian creed is formed into two integrated parts corresponding to the two bases of the people's experience. First is the Christ of creation, the eternal Image in whom all have their existence both in origin and continuity. For the human person this is the realization of natural existence within the Divine Source. As with the Johannine Hymn of Faith, the eternal Reality of Christ is asserted in a Divine Identity. Closely corresponding to the Johannine *Word*, the *Image* of Paul's teaching expresses the internal Union in which Christ can be recognized as the Incarnation of the Only Image of the True One, the Image who does not portray God (as any image attempts to do) but who is himself the Full Presence—who does not *represent* God, but who *presents* God. He is the First–born, the Only–Begotten, and it is because of him that all can exist. The phrases of universality in this creed—*the visible and the invisible, in the heavens and on earth, created through him and for him*—later become phrases of the Patristic creeds, but here they are not expressions of a philosophical cosmology. They acclaim the experience of a personal universality: everything and everyone in all their diversity and apparent petty sovereignty have meaning only in him who is "before" anything and alone keeps all in existence. It is personal not only in *him* but in *all the persons* who experience existence in him. He is not proclaimed to be the intellect's *understanding* of existence; he is celebrated by all who exist within him as they recognize him.

2   The second portion of the creed is the experience of re–creation. Paralleling the opening first acclamation *He is the Image of the Invisible God* is the acclamation of Union *He is the Head of the Body, the Gathering*. The first affirms his Identity within God, the second his identity with us. The Church, *Ekklesia*, is the gathering together of people. Literally *Ekklesia* means a gathering "out of " (*ek*–) one situation (and, by implication, gathering "into" another), but it is a gathering through "calling–by–name" (–*kleo*). We are called by name—personally, each and every individual—not gathered anonymously or as a collectivity. We are called out of one mode of existence and into another—from our natural creation into the very One in whom all find their Source of existence. Our calling–gathering is one of Union with him, a Union so complete that Paul finds the inherent organic union of the physical body to be the only realistic expression. Christ bodily alive in the Glory of Resurrection is bodily alive in the Body of per-

sons, the Gathering. It it evident from his own letters and the letters of his communities that the Gathering–Church–Ekklesia as the Resurrection Body of Christ is not intended as a metaphor. He never says the Gathering is *like* the Body of Christ. It *is* the Body. In fact we know that historically Paul is the originator of the now commonplace recognition of a *society* as a *body* of people. What becomes a general social analogy (society is like an organic body) begins in Paul's insistence that the Body of Christ *actually is people* and the Christ *who is alive now* can be found and recognized only in this Body. It is his most dynamic affirmation of the true nature of the Church: the Gathering of persons–with–persons who in Union are the living Christ in his full Resurrection. It is thus also the affirmation of the present reality of Christ: himself alive in–through–with ourselves as together we indissolubly constitute the new creation, the New Human Being.

> if we have known Christ according to the flesh
> we know him thus no longer.
> If anyone is in Christ
> he is a new creation.
> The old things have passed away—
> see! they have become new!   (II Cor. 5:16-17)

The intended literalness of the unconditioned Oneness of Christ and Gathering is clear in the central place the affirmation *the Gathering, the Body of Christ* has in this profession of Faith. It is both the parallel to the affirmation of the Divine Image and it is the pivot for the experience of Incarnation–Salvation. All come into existence through the Image, the First–born before creation; now all are drawn into reconciliation by the incarnate Fullness who gives his life and becomes the First–born from the dead so that we may be made whole in him (peace, *shalom*—"wholeness").

This is not a creed of "beliefs about Christ", it is a voicing of the actual inner experience of those who *believe* because they have *seen*. And they have seen Christ and so do not believe *about* him, they believe *in* him. They recognize him–and–themselves as they all really are in this human–Divine Union, and so they *know*. They experience being in peace, wholeness, through Christ. The ancient greeting of peace, *Shalom!*, is rooted in a word derived from the word for "whole". Christ's Peace which the world cannot give is the experience of Wholeness which can only come by Gift.

All the Fullness in him,
all reconciled to him through the Blood of the Cross:
Life Given.

SACRIFICE OF LIFE INTO GLORY

Philippians 2

5   Have that consciousness among you
    which is also that of Christ Jesus—

6   He possessed the nature of God
    yet did not cling to being equal to God,
7   but emptied himself
    taking the nature of a slave,
    born as humans are
    and found in a human way of life.
8   He humbled himself
    becoming obedient even to death,
    death on a Cross.

9   But God raised him high
    and gave him the Name beyond all names,
10 so that at the Name of Jesus
    every knee should bend—
    of heaven, on earth, and within the earth—
11 and so that every tongue should acknowledge
    Jesus Christ Lord
    to the Glory of God the Father.

1   The creed of Philippians centers on the Divinity incarnate in Jesus Christ revealed by his Sacrifice. It is prefaced by an exhortation to unity among Believers, a unity of conviction and love with one inner awareness and outlook (v.2). To be able to believe, to recognize the Truth, we must ourselves have the consciousness of Christ because we are not attempting to believe in a "truth"—we seek to recognize *him*.

Christ is experienced in a movement: from within God into human life, that life lived in open response to God and so given in sacrificial death. But that Death is the entry into new Life, into the Fullness of God now completely unveiled in Jesus so that all can recognize Him. It is an expression in two parts, Incarnation and Glorification, unified in the sacrificial act of the Gift of Life.

He is the Eternal God Who empties Himself, pours Himself out, to be an actual human being. Paul emphasizes this real humanity: He is poured into a human life so that he can give that life for us. It is in that selfless moment that the life *given* is revealed to be God *Given*.

2   And Christ receives again the Name I AM. He is revealed to be One in the Reality of God, and the ancient sign of God, the awesome Name YHWH which must never be spoken, is now his. But the Name itself is transformed: it is now the human Name Jesus, *Yeshua*, "the one who frees". God became a man, as a man gave Himself living–and–dying for us, and so entered into Glory in a Union—God–now–human is *human–now–God*. The Hidden God is now known, because we experience the meaning of the Name Jesus: *we are free*. We are freed from the slavery of death by his transformation of death.

We know that to cling to *things* can only lead to death. If *things* define who we are, then as they pass so do we. But we are *persons*, not things. We are defined by our personal uniqueness, and we can learn that we cannot be "lost" merely because of the passing away of things. If we do not act as if we depended upon things—not clinging—we begin to act in the unique power of being persons: the freedom to give and not be lost. To give to another so the other may live is an experience of the truth about ourselves. We can live only if we are free to give.

> Amen! Amen! I say to you—
> unless the grain of wheat
> falling into the ground dies,
> it remains alone
> but if it dies
> it bears much fruit.
> The one who loves his life
> will lose it;
> the one who disregards his life in this world
> will keep it in Eternal Life.   (Jn. 12:24-25)

We experience being freed in Christ: he is Given for us and so we realize we have the Power to give. Our worship is no longer directed to the image of an awesome God (however loving and merciful); we worship the One who has become one of us so that we can be free. Only this can truly proclaim the True One.

3   This is the ongoing unfoldment of revelation, the ever–extending realization of Who God fully is. This open experience is acclaimed in the recognition *Jesus Christ Lord*. For the earliest Christians this phrase itself was the most important of their creeds, for on these words depended their very lives. As the initial Roman persecutions began, the official judicial test for the treason of Christianity was the unwillingness to swear the oath formula *Caesar is Lord* (*Kyrios Kaisar*). The Roman imperial constitution depended on the principle that all human rule had been given by the gods uniquely to the Emperor; to deny this divine rule was to deny the State and Imperial Sovereignty. Christians in their inner experience of Union with Christ could not affirm Caesar to be the Lord; they recognized the One Only Lord. It was not *Kyrios Kaisar*, it was *Kyrios Iesous Christos*: to him alone should every knee bend and he alone can be acknowledged as Lord. This is the creedal formula of Paul

> No one speaking in the Spirit of God says
> *Jesus is cursed*
> and no one can say
> *Jesus is Lord*
> except by the Holy Spirit.   (I Cor. 12:3)

To proclaim Jesus Christ Lord is to affirm his Identity in God and our own unitive experience of him as he frees us. For the first Christians it was the creed which bore witness to their willingness to lay down life for the Truth. And, once again, not for an abstract truth of the mind, but for the Given True One recognized through the Spirit, the Self–Giving of God.

To accept and make our own the Gift of God in Christ is to proclaim the Glory of the Father. His Glory, the manifestation of the Power of Life, is seen in that Power alive in Christ whereby we come alive. We are free to receive the One who is poured out for us, free to give, free from what we imagine to be the need to cling and grasp, free as living persons. God's Glory is not in our awestruck silence at His Name, it is in our joy as we shout out our Freedom in the Name Jesus.

TRANSFORMATION OF CHRIST LIFE

Ephesians 3

16   In the richness of His Glory
      may He give you Power
      through His Spirit
      to grow strong in your inner self,
17   that Christ may dwell in your hearts through Faith,
      and having been rooted in and built on Love,
18   may you have strength to grasp
      with all the saints
      the breadth and length and height and depth
19   and thus know that which surpasses knowledge:
      the Love of Christ—
      so that you may be filled
      with the entire Fullness of God.

20   To Him Who can do all
      totally beyond what we ask or imagine
      through the Power at work within us,
21   to Him be the Glory
      in the Gathering
      and in Christ Jesus
      in every generation of the Age of ages.
      Amen!

1   The great Pauline prayer in Ephesians embraces both the significance of an experiential creed and the meaning of personal transformation in Christ Life. It is clearly a liturgical prayer of the Pauline communities, most probably used at the time of sacramental baptism. As the newly baptized emerges through water and the Spirit into Christ, this prayer evokes a full consciousness of Faith in the reborn and a commitment to the new Life begun now in seed and calling for a radical transformation to reach fruition in the very Fullness of God.

The prayer opens with the invocation of Glory, Power and Spirit. The Source of all that now opens as Life for the reborn is the Glory which manifests the Power of God. It is not an external sense of Power, as an exercise of domination, control or possession. This is the Power within the riches of God Himself. It is the Power of God to be God, and in no way is this a dependency on any other. To be God there is no *need* of anyone or anything else—no need to dominate, control or possess. The Power of God is the Mystery of His Selfhood: Absolute, non–relative, unconditioned, limitless, free. These, and words like them, are our recognition of Transcendence: the True Self of God is *totally unlike us, totally Other*.

The Power of God is experienced by us as "Spirit". The Absolute Self is not an abstraction of the mind. We find ourselves *moving* in response to God. The Power is Spirit, *alive*; we are affirming a Living God because we find that our own living–moving somehow reflects the Presence of God at our center of life. *Spirit, Breath, Life, Living Self* are words recognizing the Immanence of God: the True Self of God is *totally with us, totally One–All*.

We ourselves actively experience the Mystery of Transcendence and Immanence. God is simply in no way like us, and so is truly Hidden from our minds, and all our words do nothing more than proclaim this total distance of Transcendence. Yet this Hiddenness and distance from the surface of the mind in no way suggests *absence*. Our consciousness insists on the fact of Immanence: the Hidden God is absolutely present—at the center of our personhood, in the depth of the living persons we are.

And the absolute God, completely unneeding, is experienced as Gift. From the riches of His Glory, *from His Infinite Self*, He gives Power through His Spirit, *gives His Living Self*. If we attempt to imagine what it might be like if we were totally unneeding—needing no one and nothing—we immediately feel isolation. Not to need suggests a withdrawal from others, perhaps even a rejection of others. If we did not need, then we could "take them or leave them" indifferently. But the unneeding God reveals the Truth: He Who does not need is absolutely free to give. And He does not give a "thing" to fill our need, He gives Himself. Another "thing" to fill a need would merely keep us needing: both to "miss" something and to "possess" something witness to need! He gives Himself so that we can cease needing altogether, not by miraculously receiving "all things" but by being transformed, *becoming in Him as unneeding as He is*.

He gives His Living Self so that the inner self can grow strong. The Pauline prayer does not call upon God to "grow us". God is invoked to give us His Selfhood so that *we* may grow. The Gift does not render us passive and dependent. Once again, we are not given "things" to fill needs. We are given the Divine Power, and it is a true gift. The Power is now *ours* so that we ourselves can grow from within, as active and free persons.

2   Our growth in strength is growth from the Given seed of Life, Christ. He dwells in our hearts through Faith. For the ancients the heart was the symbol of the center of the person, literally the "core" (as reflected in the Latin word for heart, cor). It was not the seat of the emotions which, for the Hebrew tradition, was thought of as located within the pelvis (the "bowels of compassion"); for the Graeco–Roman tradition the emotions centered in the liver, for them the mysterious organ of divination. Christ dwelling in the heart is the Given Self of God living in the self of the human person. The two dwell in Union, the One as gift to the other so that the human begins to live in the Reality of God—Divine Life.

The dwelling in Union is by Faith. We must be alert to the Pauline experience and identification of Faith. It is not beliefs. It is *recognition*—knowing–recognizing Christ. All too often we mistake *faith* for *trust*, thinking that to believe means to accept someone else's testimony about what they (not we) have experienced. Or, Faith is trust on an even grander scale, as we imagine Faith as a "blind leap into the dark. . ." trusting that God is "there". Paul makes it quite clear that Faith is our own direct experience as we personally meet and know Christ.

> . . .do you not yourselves perceive
> that Jesus Christ is in you?   (II Cor. 13:5)

In the context of all the problems of the Corinthian community and all Paul's detailed teaching, this is the final exhortation—a proof from personal experience. It carries all the impact of the meaning of the ancient Hebrew "Amen": *Yes! It is indeed absolutely true!*

We grow strong in the Christ whom we actually experience alive in Union within us at the very core of our lives. This transforming Life has its origin in Love. Again the emphasis is upon the fundamental Reality of God revealed to us as we begin to recognize Christ: God is Love, God gives His own Self to us.

> For God so loved the world
> that He gave the Only–Begotten Son
> so that everyone who believes in him
> may not perish
> but may have Eternal Life.   (Jn. 3:16)

As the heart is the symbol of center, not emotion, so Love, *agape*, is the sign of Gift, not sentiment. We have the root of our Christ Life in this Gift, and he is the only foundation on which we can build our Christ Life. The origin of all we are and are becoming is in this Absolute Love—God Given once–for–all in the Son, God Giving continually through the Spirit.

Planting and *building* are important symbols in Paul's teaching since they lead to the sense of the beginning–point of our Christ Life through elements of our everyday experience: growing plants, building houses. The plant grows from the root as its point of origin, but in growing it becomes "more", it is not just an endless root. Yet cut off from the root it can not live. The plant–and–root together affirm the full mystery we experience: it is truly Gift, yet I am the one truly alive! Similarly, the foundation stone provides the stability of the house, but the house is shaped to match the people who are to live in it. Once again, the foundation is Gift, but we shape our lives upon it.

3   The inner deepening of life in Christ does not turn us in upon ourselves in a holy isolation. It is not and must not become a solitary mysticism. The Gift of Power, the growth of person transforming from within and the realization of Christ in Love must impel us outward. First of all, in awareness of *all the saints*—all those who share with us this One Christ Life—we cannot be *persons alone*. The Gift is made to each person individually, but it is the One Gift each receives and thus each is inescapably in Union with all others. And as we share the Selfhood of God, our sharing is *whole* in each and every participant. God in Himself cannot be received partially; the Undivided Reality must be received Whole, or not at all. Thus, as each shares it is a total sharing both in God and with others.

It is not possible to dwell realistically within Christ and be cut off from others—such is but a false imagination of the significance of Christ Life, of Faith and of inner Vision. The personal mystery of participation in Gift is the paradox of our unfolding experience: the deeper I go into Christ and the more I interiorize and the more the inner self I am grows, so much more can I look outwards and recognize all those "others" who are alive as I am—who, in fact, share completely the same Life I also completely live. As I begin to see the depth where I dwell, I find everyone else with me in depth. Thus sight opens within and I see both into the center and outward to all who are also centered there. I discover we are all growing in the One who is the All in all.

. . .you have stripped off
the old self with its practices
and have put on the new,
in full awareness of the Image
of the One Who creates him.
Here divisions have no place—
Greek and Jew,
circumcision and uncircumcision,
barbarian, Scythian,
slave, freeman—
but Christ is All and in all!   (Col. 3:9-11)

There is a second aspect to this outgoing inner vision. We see not only everyone with us in Christ, we see also the whole of reality in him. The expression is graphic: the tangible dimensions of all in their outward breadth, length, and height as well as their inward depth. This is the expression of the Incarnation of God who will be recognized only as he is, *in tangible human life*. Our inner growth in the Spirit empowers us to grasp God as Christ is. Here "grasp" has the two implications of comprehending: to be aware in consciousness, and to encompass, embrace, make one's own. We grow in Power to be able *to take* the embodied Reality of God. This is the experience of an active, not passive, living by Gift. We are not grasped by Incarnation; we grasp. Once again the experience of authentic personhood is affirmed. We are not being moved by the Spirit, we move in the Power of the Spirit, a Power now properly ours. Our re-creation into Christ Life is a Gift, but from that moment of rebirth on we are the ones alive and we are the ones with the strength to grasp. There is no thought here of a waiting for God "to do something" in our lives. There is no endless infancy of dependence. There is, rather, an unlimited openness to growth, to becoming the further person each can be as we make the Gift more and more our own, and so more and more become the One we grasp.

4   To embrace God-with-us is to grasp by Love—to see and take the One Given in the ceaseless Giving of Spirit. It entails a living-at-depth which surpasses all knowledge, for it is not an awareness in the mind *about* God-in-Christ or *about* myself in Christ Life or *about* all with me in Union. This conscious living-at-depth is consciousness as the person I am; rather than awareness about myself, it is myself self-aware. Because of Union, it

is myself self–aware in Christ and in all, as we are One. It is the total difference in the contrast: to know about someone, or to be that person and know it.

Our consciousness is Love surpassing knowledge. Because God is truly Given in Christ, in a human being just like ourselves as humans, we can reach out as persons to each other, touching and being touched. Humans can love other humans in a *human* way. This is the natural mystery of being persons: each one of us is truly unique and thus genuinely different from all others and so ununderstandable to each other as persons. Yet we find we can love each other, persons–with–persons, in a unity of lives which overcomes the potential isolation of our uniqueness. This unitive experience of love is always deeper than knowledge. In love of one another we do not merely know each other, not even know each other better or more sensitively. We begin to share what becomes a singular new life. "Two become one"—each person becoming more and more intensely *this unique person* and at the same time the persons–together becoming a new interpersonal reality, also growing more and more intensely to be *this unique unity*.

We can know–by–love the human reality of Christ, as persons in a single unitive life. And as he is One being, human–and–Divine, if we know him by love as persons, we are consciously One with the Whole Christ. Our unifying love is with God–in–Christ, the Only God Who is. In experiencing Christ we experience the Givenness of God in him to us. This is what we affirm when we then identify God as Love—*Agape*, the selfless Gift of Self. In Christ God is Given to be ours: *we are loved once–for–all.* Our experience also insists this is limitless Giving, flowing into our depth and overflowing from our depth. God is Love: absolutely Given, God loves: ceaselessly Giving. We know beyond knowledge—Love, Given in Christ Life, Giving in the Living Spirit.

As we begin to grasp, we realize that this inner experience of the Given–Giving God is our living depth. We recognize in Love that we are becoming the One we know (II Cor. 2:18). Thus in Union we ourselves further embody the Gift God is, Given in Christ, he–we together, and Giving through the Spirit our Power of new selfhood. In Incarnation God is Given, but it is an endlessly extending Incarnation, God Giving limitlessly as person after person is drawn into Christ. As we actively receive this Gift into ourselves we become the further moments of this one Incarnation, and so become the ones who are Giving what we have been Given.

Growing to know the Love of Christ beyond knowledge is therefore also our involvement in the ministry of Christ. We cannot be isolated in our inner vision since we see all others alive in the same depth. Isolation is impossible also because in Christ we reach out from our depth *to give* in the Love Given and Giving. Again, it is not possible to dwell realistically within Christ and be cut off from others. If we really have begun to know Love, then we know it is not a "thing" to be possessed. Alive in Christ, we feel the creative urge of Life ourselves: to give so that still more others may live. With all the saints we reach out to all caught up in Christ, and with them and for them come to know Love. It is vision and ministry in the same moment, because we begin to realize: there is only Gift.

5   The fruition of Christ Life begun through the Power of the Spirit is a transformation of the person resulting in nothing less than a radically new creation. For human destiny is not a merely human perfection. Rather, it is a change so fundamental that the human person is able to receive the entire Fullness of God. This limited human is to be so transformed as to encompass the unlimited God.

Christians most commonly conceive of their hoped for destiny in much humbler terms. There is a desire for a perfecting of humanity, in which somehow the negative, frustrating limitations will at last be overcome: ignorance banished, a proneness to moral failure replaced by a final commitment to the good, all need fulfilled, hurts healed. A perfected humanity would also manifest positive gifts: the sharing of an endless happiness in joy with one another, the delight in the Divine Presence drawing us close, an eternal contemplation of God revealed in His Glory with our human love responding wholly to the Love we at last recognize face-to-face. There are many traditional expressions of such expectations, but they all involve a basic characteristic: a sense of *distance* proper to the relationship of creature to Creator. However *present* we shall be to God and He to us, the absolute *separation* of Transcendence will be experienced in the absolute *difference* between ourselves and God.

But this is not the expectation of the Pauline prayer of Life. We have so changed in Christ that we shall not be merely *with God*, we shall have *God within us*. The expression is clear: we shall be filled with the Fullness— *Pleroma*. This is a word drawn from the language of the ancient mystery religions and mystical philosophy. *Pleroma* expresses Wholeness of Infinity. "Infinite" and "Unlimited" are negative words, denials of our own condition of being bounded. *Pleroma* seeks to be a positive expression of the All beyond our boundaries. It is the All experienced by mystics: not the many joined together, but the indivisible One before Whom the many individual things are as *nothings*, the One Who ultimately is All there is. It is the unitive Wholeness hinted at in even the simplest experiences of beauty, in which the person who sees or hears or touches is swept up seemingly beyond the boundaries of self and the boundaries of the beautiful thing. It is the Whole All glimpsed when wonder overwhelms us and suddenly at least for a moment we are set *free*—and *free* is the experience of beginning to be beyond boundaries, the edge of the Infinite.

To know–by–love the Self–gift of God—to receive the Given God—is to be filled with the *Pleroma*. Anything less would mean either the Gift really is not given or really is not received. If the Fullness is not Given then the gift is some "thing" and not God Himself—merely some effect felt in our lives because of God. Or if the Fullness cannot be received then there really is no gift—to be a gift, whatever is given must actually be able to become *mine*.

We receive the Power through the Spirit for the growth of our inner selves because otherwise, left to ourselves, the human person could not be filled with All God is. The Power of God–to–be–God *now ours* makes possible the Mystery of our Christ Life: to grow and so change in him that we truly become as he is.

> for in him dwells
> all the Fullness of the Godhead bodily
> and you yourselves have been filled completely in him.
>
> (Col. 2:9-10)

This transformation implies a vision of unfolding life as well as its ultimate fruition, for from the first moment of our rebirth we are becoming those able to receive Fullness. The Self–gift is Given completely in Christ as the reborn emerges from the water of the Spirit, and there is the constant Giving in the Spirit as growth in receiving that Self–gift takes place. As we more and more make the Gift our own we must inevitably begin to manifest the change within us. If in Christ we are becoming as he is, we come to act as he does. Visions of Faith and Ministry must be recognized as one. As we receive we realize we have the Power to give what is ours. This is the Ministry of Christ: the All of the Father is in the Son, this All he gives to us; we receive this All and in our turn give the All now ours to still others.

To receive the Fullness of God is totally beyond what we could ask or imagine! In the Power within us we realize the meaning of Glory, and recognize the Glory of Life in the Gathering and in Christ as Gathering and Christ are One. As Gathering, *Ekklesia*, we are all those *gathered-together*, *called-by-name* out of life into Life. This Glory is to be found only in Christ, but Christ can only be found as he now is, *with us* as we share his Life in Union. This could be neither asked for or imagined—either now as we are growing in all ways into Christ (Eph. 4:15), or at the end as we achieve the fruition of that unitive growth.

THE FULL GIFT OF GOD IN CHRIST

Ephesians 4

3 Be eager to keep the unity of the Spirit
in the bond of peace.
There is one Body and one Spirit
4 just as you were called in one hope
when you were called.
5 There is one Lord, one Faith, one baptism
6 One God and Father
of all, over all, and through all and in all.
7 But His Gift was given to each one of us,
the same as the free giving of Christ.
. . .
11 And He gave, so some are apostles,
some prophets, some evangelists,
some shepherds, and some teachers
12 for the perfecting of the saints
in the work of serving
in building up the Body of Christ,
13 until we all attain the unity of Faith
and the full awareness of the Son of God—
until we are a completely mature Human Being
as measured by the stature
of the Fullness of Christ.

1   The meaning for Life of the great Prayer and its ultimate expectations are further expressed in the solemn exhortation of Paul. The unity of the Spirit is experienced in peace—*shalom*, "wholeness"—the peace which binds us together. Together we are a single Body, the living Resurrection Christ Given in the ever–growing Incarnation embracing us all. It is a single Spirit we share, reborn through the endless Self–Giving of God. This is our hope, the one expectation of the meaning of our lives now transformed into One Life: the Only Lord whom we are increasingly able to recognize because we truly have been born again through water and Spirit.

We begin to respond to the One God Who is thus revealed as Abba. But He is not *our* Father in any narrow, possessive sense. Our response to Him is in love because we have experienced Love absolutely: He pours Himself out into all that all might live. The expression is dramatic—He is Father *of* all, *over* all, *through* all, *in* all (—if there are more ways to insist on His universal Self–gift, then add those as well!). Each and every one of us receives this Gift and its measure is the same as the free, selfless giving we have experienced in Christ: he gave himself without conditions to all, he gave demanding nothing not even that he be received, he gave *loving*.

2   As we receive this Gift we enter Union with Christ and so take up his Sacred Work, Re–Creation, and we begin to minister Life in all the distinctive ways which reflect our distinctive individualities. All build up the One Body, the living Reality of Christ we share, and we come into increasing consciousness of our Union, ultimately recognizing the Son as he is: *with us*. Our transformation is completed as we become that single Human Reality grown to maturity. The Pauline tradition does not speak of us becoming *many* perfected human beings—in Christ we are person–with–person One New Human. And this single maturity is the Fullness of Christ. The original words express this clearly: in our personal growth into Christ we will become the *mature* Human, *teleion*, a maturity to be measured by the *Fullness* of Christ, *pleromatos*. *Teleion* implies a *growth into completion*, stage by stage; *pleromatos* implies a reality *already complete* as integrally whole and indivisible. We *become complete* in the singular humanity of Christ who is himself the embodiment of *Fullness* as the Incarnation of All God is. Our Union is Two–fold: human person–with–person and human–Divine.

THE GATHERING: CHRIST IN FULLNESS

Ephesians 1

17 May the God of our Lord Jesus Christ,
    the Father of Glory,
    give you a Spirit of wisdom
    and revelation of a full consciousness of Him.
18 enlightening the eyes of your hearts
    so you can know
    what is the hope of His calling,
    what is the richness of the Glory
    in His inheritance for the saints,
19 and what is the overwhelming greatness
    of His Power for believers,
    exercised in the strength of His might
20 which He worked in Christ
    raising him from the dead
    and seating him at His right hand in the heavens
21 beyond all rule and authority
    and power and lordship
    and any name that can be named,
    not only in this age
    but also in that yet to come
22 *He has put all things under his feet*,
    and as head of all things
    He gave him to the Gathering
    which is his Body,
    the fullness of him who fills all with All.

1   Complementing the great baptismal prayer of Paul is another prayer
embodying an experiential creed. As we see with the creed in Colossians,
there are phrases here which will appear in the later Patristic philosophical
creeds. But, once again, the appeal in belief here is not to the mind through
statements expressing ideas about a revelation of Christ. It is to *the eyes
of your hearts*, the inner insight of the *person* as the unitive consciousness
of another person arises.

We are given a Spirit bringing us to a *full consciousness of Him, to know His Power as we experience being overwhelmed* by it as the Power of Life—raising Christ, glorifying him, uniting all to him in the Gathering, his Body: the Full Christ who fills all with All.

The Gathering as *the fullness of him who fills all with All* goes literally infinitely beyond the image of the ancient community as the *People of God*. The community in Christ is not a people enjoying a particular relationship to God, as defined for Israel at Sinai: agreeing to observe the commands of the Torah, this people enters a covenant to be a people dedicated to YHWH alone, and He enters the covenant to be their God, theirs beyond any other people's. The covenant is an agreement entailing an exchange—dedication to YHWH with observance of Torah in exchange for Presence in Power with the endless promise of Salvation. The very form of the covenant is an ancient form of contract among merchants, and thus expresses the relationship entered as clearly external, one party relating in a specified way to another.

This is not at all the relationship of Christ and all called into him, the Gathering. Those called–by–name into him form with him an integral Union: they, the many, have become One. The relationship is in no way external—one relating *to* another. The relationship is unitive—all together share a *single interpersonal identity*. If Christ is truly God–in–Gift filling all with All, then those filled are now truly the fullness of Christ. In the experience of Gift there can be no agreement for an exchange—gifts cannot be bought and sold! In Gift there can be only *free–giving* and *free–receiving*. The ancient covenant experience could be but a bare hint of what could be by Gift. The covenant pointed toward unity by relating the human to the Divine; Christ is himself the human–Divine Union, and Christ fully is the Christ–Gathering, the endlessly extending Union person–with–person.

Again, as with all the expressions of the experience of Faith by the earliest Christians, this realization of Union is not to be a selfish sense of triumph. If indeed the Gathering is his fullness, then the entire community *must be* fully *why* he is our Union: to give Life. It is a ministering community who experience being the fullness as we begin to experience–by–serving, as we minister through our concrete lives with all our varied tangible acts, and thus incarnationally *fill all with All*.

four

MINISTRY:
THE GIFT OF BLESSINGS

INTRODUCTION

1   The Matthean communities of Jewish Christians experienced their
Faith as the fulfillment of lives formed through the experience of Torah.
Moses had led Israel from captivity to freedom, and at Sinai had been the
messenger bringing the Torah, the sacred gift of the pattern for life: if people
lived each day choosing to follow the commands they would grow to realize
the true meaning of their lives. The Law commanded only what was best
for humankind, as would be discovered in the free response of obedience.
Moses taught the observance of Torah and it was received as the gift which
led to what life could become. The first Christians discovered that Torah
had led them to a new opening of life.

Jesus their Teacher had drawn them into his own life. They awoke in
Faith to recognize him: this actual man Jesus and the Fullness of All God
is are completely One in Union. And they recognized themselves: each
transformed to participate in that Union. They looked back now and
understood how they had been made ready for this rebirth. They had been
taught by Moses the vision of human perfection and in Jesus they had found

its embodiment. He had taught them how to enter the New Life to which a purely human perfection could be but the threshold. Moses taught the path of life, and it led them to Christ. In Christ they found the New Gift: *the Living God Himself given to us so we may live in Him.*

For the Matthean communities Moses the Teacher of Israel was the prophetic sign of Christ. As Moses had gathered Israel at the foot of Sinai to receive the gift of Torah, so Jesus gathers his disciples to him on the mount to receive his Gift. Moses and Sinai in the desert foreshadow Jesus and a hill in the countryside. But the awesomeness of a God hidden beyond thundering clouds gives way to the simplicity of God–with–us. The call to obedience to a plan of life gives way to the invitation to enter Divine Life. The gift of Torah had been the Law of Commandments, the New Gift is Blessings.

2   In times when human relationships are often shallow the real meaning of *blessing* is easily lost. We may come to think of it as mere words—a benevolent well–wishing towards others, literally "speaking well" or "saying kind things". But if relationships are deep and not shallow then the *act of blessing* is a dynamic reality arising from within a deep person who reaches out to another to give a gift–of–life.

For ancient peoples the giving of a blessing was at the heart of the transmission of life. The first blessing in the Torah is given in the midst of the creation story: God affirms that the work of each day is good, and then with the creation of the fish and birds

> God blessed them, saying:
> Be fruitful, multiply and fill the waters in the seas and let the
> birds multiply on the earth!   (Gen. 1:22)

The first blessing is the gift of the power to create further life. The second blessing is given to the first man and woman, the power to create new life and to have dominion over all the things of their lives. The third blessing is the gift of the Sabbath Day, the power of bringing works to their completion and so to enter the rest of fulfillment.

In the story of Jacob and Essau the ancient sense of the reality of blessing is vivid in the agony of its loss. Jacob has tricked his aged father Isaac into giving him the blessings which should go to his older brother: he receives the blessings of the sky's rain and earth's richness, rule over peoples and over all the family, and "cursed be they who curse you, and blest be they who bless you!" When Essau comes to Isaac and they realize what Jacob has done, Essau cries "He stole my birthright and now he has stolen my blessing. Have you not kept a blessing for me?...Do you have only one blessing, father?" But all had been given to Jacob. (Gen. 27)

In the religious life of ancient Israel under Torah the hereditary priests, the descendants of Aaron, had been given the power to bless the people with God's blessing from the Sanctuary.

> The Lord spoke to Moses and said:
> Say this to Aaron and his sons—
> This is how you are to bless the sons of Israel.
> You shall say to them:
> May the Lord bless you and keep you,
> May the Lord let His Face shine upon you and be gracious to you,
> May the Lord show His Face to you and bring you peace.
> This is how you are to invoke My Name
> on the sons of Israel
> and I will bless them.   (Num. 6:22-27)

The priests blessed daily life with the Power of God's Name, His Presence. After the Roman destruction of the Temple, the Rabbinic Tradition taught that until the Sanctuary could be rebuilt in Jerusalem none of the sacred rites could be performed. But the gift of the priesthood must not be lost, and so at the close of the Sabbath service in the synagogue all the descendants of the priests in the congregation come forward and raise their hands over the others in the priestly blessing (spreading their fingers in such a way as to symbolize the Hebrew letter *shin*, for the sacred Name *Shaddai*, the All–Powerful, from Whose creative Power all life–gifts come).

The Hebrew word *baruk*, with its Greek counterpart *eulogetos*, expresses the fact of being *blest*: having received the gift of God. It can also express (as *barak*) the human response to God, the thankful praise for gifts, "may the Lord be blest". We are blessed and so respond to the Source of our blessing. The Hebrew word *ashre*, with its Greek counterpart *makarios*, expresses the human state of happiness or "blessedness" which is ours as we receive, recognize and share our gifts. In the New Gift of Blessings each of the Blessings expresses the Gift of Christ and so the one gifted is proclaimed "blessedly happy"—*ashre, makarios.*

3   To bless, one must have the *power to bless.* It is the power to give, ultimately the inmost Power of God Who gives Himself. The person who blesses gives from within, giving gifts the person truly possesses. To bless with words only—mere well-wishing—betrays the shallowness of the person: no gifts are found within, there is nothing to give but words without depth. But *to bless with power* is *to give* from the depths of a living person.

Jesus blesses all who are drawn to him—men, women and children. They are blessed with the two-fold Power to dwell within the inner Reality of God, and so to enter into the further work of creation—the transformation/transfiguration/resurrection of all in Christ. They are blessed by being awakened in Faith to begin to see themselves in this new creation. It is Faith as actually-experienced consciousness, not a blind leap. It is the Faith of people who experience the living Union of God-in-Christ-in-us. And they are blessed by being moved in Love to serve others in life-sharing. It is Love in the experience of self-giving in deep freedom. It is the Love of people more and more at One with the God Who pours Himself out completely.

As Jesus gives his Blessings we experience the real test of Faith and Love, dwelling and co-creating within God. Each Blessing identifies *who we must be* to be able *to do*—the living Power is not a mindless principle, but the conscious reality of actual persons.

Matthew 5

1   And seeing the crowds he went up the mount,
and sitting, his disciples gathered around him.
2   And beginning to speak he taught them, saying—

THE FIRST BLESSINGS: POWER TO GIVE

3   The poor-in-spirit are blessedly happy,
for theirs is the Kingdom of Heaven.
4   The gentle are blessedly happy,
for they shall inherit the earth.

1   The giving of the Kingdom of Heaven and the inheritance of the earth are two expressions of the same gift. To inherit the earth *in Christ* is not to be enriched by *possessing* (the exclusiveness of ownership) nor by *dominating* (the subjugation of overlordship). Christ reveals God not as possessor or dominator but as the One Who *gives*, and gives absolutely: He so loves the world that He gives His One Son that we may live and live fully.

God does not *possess* anything—he does not *need*; we seek to possess things because we do need. Each of us exists within limits and so we must seek all that we lack. When we affirm *God is limitless* (the Infinite) we must not imagine God as "possessing all things" and thus "lacking nothing". Such an image is only an image of ourselves as gigantic human beings devouring all things: this would be a god needing everything and hence slave to all! We need—God does not!

The human image of a god who needs and possesses is an idol. Christ, the True Image of God, reveals *Gift*. God, truly limitless, is absolutely free: free of needing anything or anyone, and thus *free to give*.

We can always be tempted by the false image of possessing. We imagine God is God because of some *thing*, some principle or power, He has and we do not. And so if we too could come to possess "it" we would indeed become as "gods" (Gen. 3:5). But God is God precisely because He depends on nothing: in Himself He absolutely IS. In ourselves we cannot become as "gods" because we must *have*: we depend on everything and everyone.

2   We can become as God is by the transformation of receiving God's Self-gift. By becoming One with Him as He is *Given* in Christ, we grow in the Power of the Spirit until we can be filled with the complete Fullness of God (Eph. 3:19). To be blessed with the Kingdom of Heaven and the inheritance of the earth is not to possess them and so be fulfilled by them. Rather, we are empowered to enter the Self-giving Who is God and, at One within Him, *give—give* the Kingdom of Heaven: the Divine Power of New Life; *give* the earth: re-create all things to bring them to their real fulfillment, at One-with-us-within-Him.

This is the two-fold Blessing of the poor-in-spirit, the gentle. The poor-in-spirit are those who discover they do not need to possess or dominate. The persons and things of their daily lives are recognized to be gifts, coming freely and remaining free. They may be involved with many things or with few; they care for their gifts and show responsible concern in improving their potentials for life. But they remain poor-in-spirit if all the richness of gifts always means *the power to give*. And so they are gentle: they have no need to dominate, they can only truly give if they can give freely and if those who receive can take freely.

The gentle poor–in–spirit bear witness to God in the meaning of life. God gives: Himself, absolutely, without reservation or condition, without even the presumption that His Gift will be received. The gentle poor–in–spirit bear witness to the wonder: not that we love and receive God, but that God first loves us, gives to us (I Jn. 4:10). The gentle poor–in–spirit bear witness that there is

> One God and Father
> of all, over all, through all and in all.
> His Gift comes to each of us
> in the same manner as the free–giving of Christ.   (Eph. 4:6-7)

The gentle poor–in–spirit are blessed with everything—heaven and earth—by being blessed with Christ Life: all the Fullness of the Godhead dwelling bodily in him–us.

THE SECOND BLESSINGS:
GIFT OF POWER

5   Those who mourn are blessedly happy,
    for they shall be comforted.
6   Those hungering and thirsting for justice are blessedly
    happy,
    for they shall be satisfied.
7   The compassionate are blessedly happy,
    for they shall receive compassion.

1   The gentle poor–in–spirit are blessed to be able to give heaven and earth. Filled in Christ, they give the Power of Life and the Fulfillment of all things re–created in him. Their witness, therefore, is not to be passive. In the midst of the human family it is to be a powerful and creative gift, bringing a further three–fold Blessing in the struggle for the truth of life.

There is suffering in the human family. Between birth and death we all experience the tensions and contradictions of actual living. As we are truly individuals we know the fact of limit and need, and as we are truly persons–with–persons we know the act of seeking one another. We find both meaning and meaninglessness, satisfaction and frustration.

In the midst of human suffering is the experience of evil. Beyond the fact that we are not "gods" is the destructiveness of which we are capable. Limit and need can suggest: take, possess, exclude. Seeking one another can suggest: control, manipulate, dominate. Meaning can be mere self-assertion. Meaninglessness can be rejection of others. Satisfaction can be nothing more than pride. Frustration can be the fear that commands us to hate.

It is not enough to be gentle poor–in–spirit. We must mourn the presence of evil in life. It should not be and it need not be. Those who destroy twist the gift of life they have received. Only if we are struck *it must not be,* can we receive the Blessing of being comforted. Those who mourn the evil destroying lives are comforted with the Blessing of vision: *it shall not be!*

2   This Blessing is a vision of the present, not of a distant future. If the destruction of lives is truly mourned, then there is a hunger and thirst for all that life should be. Within human creative powers we know we *can* create ways of life which recognize and honor the unique gift each person is and what the sharing of interpersonal life together can mean for all. We can know both the ideal and practice of justice. Only if *at least some* men and women are consumed with a passion for justice will any receive justice. The thirsting and hungering for the sake of others as they cry out in need is a commitment of the power of persons to the powerless persons. Those who are not powerless give themselves so that others may live.

Not to be powerless cannot be defined only in terms of things—the things which can be concretely used to right wrongs and restore the value of individuals and communities. The power of persons is that which arises within the inner self–identity: the willingness *to give of one's self*, not merely to give the things one possesses. The powerless are those who have been deprived of that inner sense. They have lost their sense of freedom, worth, and dignity. If they are truly powerless their loss is infinitely more intense than any loss of tangible things: they have been abandoned. And so their full restoration must be as persons, through the only real power we possess, the power to commit ourselves as persons to one another—even, and especially, when we have no tangible means to fulfill the call to justice.

3   Our mourning, our hungering and thirsting, must be rooted in our own experience of inner unity with those we would serve. It is not enough to be moved by suffering, nor to act that those who suffer might be restored. To be blessed with the gift of justice and be able to so bless others, we must enter the lives of those who suffer. We must be the compassionate, not merely the benign helpers.

In Hebrew the word for compassion, *rakham*, derives from the same root as the word for womb. These words point us to the ancient experience of human unity. For every individual born of woman arises into life, takes substance, shape, nurture, and depends totally *within* another. Our unremembered formative experience is an individual—myself—in complete union with another. It is an experience unremembered, yet it is actually *in our bones*. We are forever a living memory of *life-together*: two individuals distinctly themselves yet also intimately one. Every one of us comes into existence through this same experience. Every one of us, then, has the built-in power of living unity. And every one of us can know the meaning of the Blessing of compassion: entering into and sharing life with another.

Mourning and hungering–thirsting for justice without compassion cannot be the blessings they should be. For without the true giving of self as a personal sharing with others, our sense of justice will be an idea only and those who suffer will be "others" to us. Without a person–consciousness, justice and injustice are nothing more than concepts, however ideal, of legal relationships fulfilled or violated. Without a person–consciousness our passion for even idealistic legal justice easily becomes the fanaticism of commitment to a theory of human society. Unless we see ourselves ultimately *one* with others, they and their needs become *objects*. And left to itself zeal for objects can transform us into sources of human evil: those who *possess* the proper pattern for life, who *control* life's possibilities, who *manipulate conformity* to our vision.

To mourn suffering is a gift. To hunger and thirst for all that is right is a gift. To be compassionate, entering personally and sharing with others in their need so that we and they are one, is a gift. These three Blessings together are the gift of our full commitment to one another, as those blessed with the freedom of all that comes from God: the gentle poor–in–spirit loving one another.

THE THIRD BLESSINGS: VISION IN UNION

8   The pure in heart are blessedly happy,
     for they shall see God.
9   The peacemakers are blessedly happy,
     for they shall be called sons of God.

1   The Lord is One, there is no other. He is, in Himself, Undivision. He alone absolutely IS. In Christ we awaken to the wonder: God Given to us, given as He is in Himself—complete Self-gift. If He gives Himself, God must give Himself completely. He does not exist by possessing anything not Himself. He does not exist in dimensions, aspects or moments. There is no "divine thing" we could be given. There is no "portion" which could become ours. The One-Only God gives the One-All that God is.

Only if we are undivided persons—whole in the commitment at the center of our lives—can we see God as He really is. We cannot commit ourselves to God and all His creation loved in Him and at the same time be turned in upon ourselves selfishly, loving only to take. We cannot serve two masters. We must be whole-hearted to be open to the Fullness of God. In the Gift of Christ we can be healed of our divisions. We can become whole within, our lives centered on God alone. This is the first and greatest of the commandments.

> Hear, O Israel, the Lord our God, the Lord is One!
> And you shall love the Lord your God
> with all your heart
> and with all your soul
> and with all your mind
> and with all your strength.   (Mk. 12:29-30)

And, as we become whole with all others in the life we share:

> You shall love your neighbor as yourself.
> There is no commandment greater than these.   (Mk. 12:21)

We can grow to see the Invisible God made visible in His Son, the Only True Image—the Image who embodies God, incarnate in actual human life.

In this is Love:
not that we have loved God
but that He has loved us
and sent His Son as sacrifice for our sins.
Beloved, if God has so loved us
we also ought to love one another.
No one has ever seen God—
if we love one another God dwells in us
and His Love is brought to perfection in us.   (I Jn. 4:10-12)

2   As we are healed and become whole in Christ in our inmost selves, and begin to live shared lives, we are blessed with the gift of vision.

The Hebrew word for peace, *shalom*, is rooted in the experience of wholeness, not tranquility. One who comes in peace, who embodies peace and thus can bring peace is the one who is *whole* within and seeks to share this gift. Peacemaking—*wholeness making*—is needed where there is division, violence, tension. The peacemaker comes with the power to heal and so does not expect to live in tranquility. Wholeness within is the inner strength which makes it possible to dwell at the very center of the tensions of life and not be engulfed by them but, on the contrary, be the beginning of their resolution.

Jesus is the man of peace, and he is anything but quiet or passive. He has come to bring a sword cutting away all that is false, for the tension of leading divided lives must be resolved that all may become whole-hearted. He desires that all the world be set afire, to be consumed as a holocaust sacrifice and transformed into the Sacred.

The peacemakers are whole themselves through the Gift of Union in God and so can bring that Wholeness Who is the One-All to others. They are blessed to see God and be seen as God's true offspring.

THE FOURTH BLESSINGS:
TRIUMPH OF THE CROSS

10   Those who are persecuted in the cause of justice are
        blessedly happy,
        for theirs is the Kingdom of Heaven.

11   When they reproach you and persecute you
      and say all evil, lying against you for my sake
      you are blessedly happy:
12   Rejoice and be glad!
      because your reward is great in heaven,
      for thus they persecuted the prophets before you.

1   The gentle poor–in–spirit, who mourn for those who suffer, who hunger
and thirst for the righting of wrongs and who serve compassionately, they
who see God and are recognized to be God's own offspring as the whole-
hearted bringers of peace—these who are blessed with all of heaven and
earth—must be willing to accept this final Blessing. But it seems so illogical.
They have come to realize so much of the true meaning of human life as
they have committed themselves to the Gift of God in Christ. And they
have been blessed with everything. In them dwells the Fullness of the
creative Power of God, the very Spirit of Life. Yet they must expect rejection and apparent failure in their selfless commitment, and recognize the
presence of a Blessing: the triumph of the Cross—that Love which is God
himself.

God in Christ gives Himself to us freely. And because the giving really
is *giving* it really is free, both in God and in us. Only God is Fullness. He
is the All–in–all, not as an infinite accumulation of a countless *many*, but
as the limitless whole Oneness. It is from within His unique inner Reality
that He gives, not *something* but His Whole Self. And so He gives freely
because He alone can give completely and not be wasted or diminished
or lost. He gives Himself freely and thus gives *for no reason*—without any
demands, with no return, nothing needed—not even that His giving be
received.

His giving in us is truly free as we do receive. There is no condition
set for our receiving. The gift is ours even before we realize it, for it is in
God's Self-giving that we receive our very existence. We *are* because God
loves–gives, and God simply loves–gives freely. We receive freely because
His giving is truly Love as it really can be, actual Self-giving. Because it
is Love we receive, we experience our freedom.

There is no fear in love
but perfect Love casts out fear,
because fear has torment

and the one who fears
has not been perfected in Love.
We love because He first loved us.   (I Jn. 4:18-19)

2   God gives Himself before we can receive. We do not understand why, but some receive Him—actively embrace His giving—immediately. For others their response is yet to come. And for still others the response is a rejection—or so it appears, even to them. We must recognize in all of these the signs of our freedom. God's giving is not a disguise for compulsion.

If His giving is rejected it is not a *thing* rejected, but Himself. And those who have received Him and so have been received in that Self become so One with Him that they too must be rejected. If Christ is received, all in him are received; if Christ is rejected, so are all who are his. Those who are in Christ seek only to partake of God's Self–giving to all—as they dwell in Him they do not seek a limited, unfree giving, a giving conditioned upon a receiving.

A God Who gives freely, demanding nothing either before or after, can seem foolish and powerless to those who cannot receive freely. If we believe we can only be fulfilled by possessing and dominating, then the Christ who pours out his Life for all is mad and must be destroyed, for his Life–giving denounces the lie of our self–deception. And those who have already received his Gift are the living witnesses who spread his madness and must be destroyed with him.

We preach Christ crucified. . .
a Christ who is the Power of God
and the Wisdom of God.
For the foolishness of God
is wiser than the wisdom of humans,
and the weakness of God
is stronger than the power of humans. . .
By God's doing you are in Christ Jesus,
who by God's doing has become
our wisdom, our uprightness,
our holiness and our freedom,
so that as has been written:
If anyone would boast,
let him boast in the Lord.   (I Cor. 1:23-25,30)

3   The mystery of rejection is encountered throughout all of life. One person turns away from another. Where people should be hearing the call to fulfill human life they can bring division. Conflict over things, great or petty, so easily entraps us into making persons over into things. For *things* can be rejected in favor of other things, and often with high motives. Persons *as persons* cannot be rejected without exposing our own sense of being person to the same danger.

> Indeed, the hour is coming
> when everyone who kills you
> will believe he is offering service to God!
> And they will do these things
> because they did not know
> either the Father or me.   (Jn. 16:2-3)

Yet those who reject are not themselves rejected! They have not known the Gift—they have not recognized the Person Given—but the giving still takes place. At the central moment of life–death–resurrection, as Jesus pours out his human life so that all may have Life in him, he prays

> Father forgive them:
> they do not know what they are doing.   (Lk. 23:34)

The Blessing of sharing in his rejection is not a test of faithfulness. It is not a negative sacrifice demanded by God as a condition for His Gift. God makes no demands, sets no conditions. This Blessing is the human reality of the freedom of the Gift. To be willing to receive this Blessing is to receive the Power to create Life with God.

> When a woman gives birth she suffers
> because her hour has come.
> But when she brings forth the child
> she no longer remembers the pain
> because of her joy
> that a human being has been born into the world.   (Jn. 16:21)

five

PRAYER:
VISION—RECOGNITION

PRAYER AS CONSCIOUSNESS

1   Our own awakening of consciousness within Christ as we actually experience sharing his Life is prayer. As the Mind of Christ is not ideas about ideas—but the personal recognition *who he–we are within the Self–Gift of God*—so prayer is not its forms or words. Prayer as consciousness is the response to Christ Life: *intensively* within Christ the Source, and *extensively* in the unitive experience which reaches out to others as we recognize one another as we all draw One Life from that Source.

Words and forms give momentary shape to this prayer–consciousness within each individual, and the shapes affirm the integrity and uniqueness of the person: *I am the one praying in this concrete moment of my life*. But the shapes do not confine prayer within these forms or words, or ultimately within the individual alone, for words spoken together open our prayer–consciousness to one another. *Prayers* are moments in the flowing process of prayer, and *prayer* is the experienced consciousness of sharing Christ Life.

Prayer as consciousness affirms the inner reality of the individual person. *Prayer as sharing* affirms the interpersonal unity of the One Christ.

2   Matthew 18

19   Again, Amen! I say to you:
     if two of you on earth
     agree on anything at all to ask,
     it shall be granted to you
     by my Father in Heaven.
20   For where two or three are gathered
     in my Name
     I am there in their midst.

In the tradition of the Torah the agreement of two witnesses is suffi-
cient testimony to the truth of any issue. Christ promises that if two of
his followers are at one in anything they seek it will be granted because
of their shared witness that truly it is needed for Life. But he draws us beyond this image of the two witnesses who approach God in supplication.
As we *come and see* Christ Life from within, we recognize we are not together simply as witnesses. We are "two or three" who even in the smallest
numbers constitute a community of persons sharing with Christ. We do
not *approach* God—we have been *gathered into* Christ. And what we are
conscious of as needed for Life we will learn in him.

In Christ we are always in community. At the very least the individual
who prays is in Union with the full individual Jesus Christ, person–with–
person. Further, whether or not we advert to it, this same person–with–
person Union is shared with all other individuals called into Christ Life.
Together we are member–for–member the living resurrection Body of Christ:
he in us, we in him, so the world will be able to realize he–we dwell in
the Father and the Father in us. In the growing experience of prayer the
full meaning of sharing Life unfolds as we begin the process of recognizing: the unique personal identity *Jesus Christ*, known by *me* a unique person, as I come to experience the fact of *Union*, discovering all the other
unique persons *called together* in Christ.

We are not just two or three who associate together. We are gathered,
and the original word *synegmenoi* suggests the process of being drawn
together in the catching of fish by the dragnet or in the winnowing of wheat
with the kernels heaped together. Such gathering implies a sense of separation: drawn from old relationships into new.

3   The new relationship is expressed in the ancient sense of the power of names. Names are words that point not to things or ideas but to persons. As each person *as person* is unique, the name can never tell us *about* the person since uniqueness allows no comparisons or contrasts. Name celebrates the mystery of each inner–self person, and implies a call to recognizing *here I am!*

Ancient and primitive peoples have felt this mystery of person as awesome, even dangerous, and so have invested names with a sense of power. To know a person's name was to enter into the depths of who that unique person really is. Thus the celebration of person implied in a name could have its dark side, a fear of attempts to gain power over the inner–self by magical use of the name. And so Moses is depicted (Ex. 3:13–15) as seeking to know the real name of God—the people will insist on being told the Divine Name and hence be able to invoke it with power. But Moses is rebuffed: he is told simply *ehyeh asher ehyeh*, "I am What I am". God gives a Name which does not reveal His inner Selfhood, but reaffirms His inner Mystery always unknowable and hidden beyond any words, even names.

Those gathered into Christ are gathered into his Name. They are not just two or three assembled by virtue of Christ's authority or mandate. They are together in his Name: in his own inner–self of personal existence, sharing in his unique identity, in the Power of what it is for him to exist in his Fullness. It is in this that the community in prayer within Christ is totally beyond the image of the two witnesses testifying to a need to be brought in prayer to God. Prayer within Christ is indeed *within* him: those gathered in his Name discover he really is in their midst. But this means much more than an accompanying presence. The original words for "midst", *en meso*, call upon us to recognize he is at our *center*, the unifying Person who is the experienced Power of the One Life we share. If three of us are gathered in his Name he is not with us simply as a fourth individual. We dwell in him and he in us, *just as* he and the Father dwell truly One. (Jn. 17:23)

4   To pray is to participate consciously in that inmost Reality of Christ we experience as Life. We each participate as an authentic person, yet our participation together–with–him is the transformation from life to Life, in which we discover we have become One New Human Being (Eph. 4:13). This is a complete Union in Christ, yet without any hint of a destruction or diminution of any individuality. We are simultaneously *unique persons* and also *the unique and new "interperson"* of Christ Life. These paradoxes

state the Mystery: our lives are hidden in the Life of Christ in whom is hidden the Eternal Mystery. But we are drawn to consciousness within Christ as he reveals the Mystery in his own Person. To know the *Mystery who is Christ–in–us* (Col. 1:27) we must come and see where he lives, and to enter the Mystery we must live where we find him alive—in–through–with one another *at our shared center.*

5   Matthew 6

    16   But when you pray
         go into your inner room
         and having shut the door
         pray to your Father
         Who is in that secret place
         and your Father Who sees in secret
         will reward you.

For ancient Israel the realization of the hiddenness of God never suggested either a remoteness from human affairs or an irrelevance to the human mind. The always–hidden God was manifested through His Presence in Power, and that Power could be approached. Yet the expectations bound up in any attempt to approach God were explicitly limited. The Power of God was not manifested in every human situation—hence the anguish so common throughout the Psalms in waiting for the comings of the Lord to restore justice, heal suffering, end exile. In prayer true wisdom was rooted in awe of the All–Powerful, and regardless of how confident the seeker was of divine favor, he was also vividly aware of the ultimate gulf separating creature and Creator. This gulf was ritualized dramatically in the Temple itself, in its courts, walls and entries. The uncircumcised could approach only as far as the outermost court; the women of Israel stopped at their court, while the men could proceed to the next; beyond that only the Levites were admitted; finally the priests entered the Holy Place of the Temple each day to offer the Prayer of Incense before the veiled and forbidden Holy of Holies, the *Debir*, the "Inner Room"—here once each year the High Priest entered to sprinkle the blood of Atonement upon the Ark, the "footstool" of God's throne set upon the firmament. The ritual celebration of God's Presence in Power also expressed His absolute separation.

To pray within Christ is to enter our own inner room, the All–Holy *Debir*, the Center of our own inner personal presence—a secret place, hidden from all others because of the uniqueness of each person. In Christ we discover *this* is the Inner Room of God. He dwells in the secret place: the hiddenness of self. And He sees in secret: the lives hidden in the Life who is Christ. And once again we confront our unity in the Mystery: each one enters the secret place of person, and in coming to recognize this is the Inner Room of God's Presence in Power, we each recognize all the others who also have entered with Christ once–for–all into the One Holy of Holies.

To pray within Christ is at once an intense act of individuality and the opening consciousness of community. It is the experiencing–in–depth of one's self, of the individual Jesus Christ, and of all those individual selves in Union with him. It is also the experiencing of God in His Depth of Self, as God and Man are Truly One in Jesus Christ—to see him *is* to see the Father (Jn. 14:9).

PRAYER AS THE MIND OF CHRIST

Luke 11

1   And once he was in a certain place praying.
     And when he was finished one of his disciples said:
     Master, teach us to pray,
     just as John taught his disciples.
2   And he said to them: When you pray, say:
     Father!
     may Your Name be proclaimed Holy,
     may Your Kingdom come;
3   give us each day our daily bread,
4   and forgive us our sins
     for we ourselves forgive everyone in debt to us,
     and do not bring us to the test.

1   In living with Christ the first disciples have often seen him at prayer, and they realize *when Jesus prays it is not like the prayer of others*. Their own experience of prayer has been formed within one of the great traditions

of prayer—the Psalms and Songs of the Hebrew Scriptures, the Temple Liturgy, the synagogue houses of prayer where the faithful celebrate the Sabbath in the offering of prayer. And some have been taught the prayer of preparation by John—repentance and expectation. But the prayer of Jesus is like none of these. They see him experiencing God in a new way, and they seek to enter that way themselves. They are not asking instruction in a prayer discipline (this they have had from childhood). They want to pray just as Jesus prays.

2   *When you pray, say: Father!*

The depth–center of Jesus' consciousness throughout his ministry is his recognition of God as *Father*. Over and over the Gospels record Jesus expressing his relationship with God as son with father. And in his instruction and prayer he taught his followers that they too must recognize God as their Father. In the context of the Tradition of Israel this marks a striking departure: God no longer approached in awe—God embraced!

The word Jesus used was *Abba*. In the development of the Aramaic language from the older Semitic languages (including Hebrew), the word for "father" took form as the diminutive *abba* (literally "daddy"). The Hebrew word *ab* means "father", but with the formal overtones of "father". We may speak the word father with great warmth and affection but there always remains a sense of dignity and reverence. The Aramaic abba is a word of love and delight, completely devoid of formality. It arose in the context of Semitic family life, in which the very young are doted upon by their parents; small children can do no wrong (though they might have to be snatched away from their mischief for their own sakes); children are the gift of life, and life is to be enjoyed boundlessly with them as they play and laugh, and as they nestle asleep in their parents' arms. And thus the delight of children in their father who loves them, hugs them, laughs with them—a delight expressed in the child's word abba. It is a word of total intimacy, an innocence of love and trust.

Jesus speaks of and to God with this child–word Abba. He does not use any of the formal and ritual modes of address canonized in the Tradition of his people. He *always* and *exclusively* says Abba. Nowhere in the Tradition of Israel can we find a parallel. He alone proclaims God Abba.

We cannot appreciate the shock experienced by his original hearers. Although in a few instances the Hebrew Scriptures speak of God as Father, these are clearly poetic metaphors (comparable to Hosea speaking of God as the Husband of Israel). And God as *Father* is *Ab*, with its appropriate implication of reverence. To speak of God as *Abba-Daddy* is blasphemous— unless it is true—since it reveals the consciousness of the speaker: God and I are One in my identity as true Son.

With all the difficulties we have in attempting to assess the inner consciousness of Jesus–the–man in his Divine Reality (how he knew his identity within the human process of experience and emergent awareness), of one thing we can be certain: *he recognized God as his Abba*. And this necessarily manifests his own self–recognition. In the Gospel accounts this is the ultimate reason for his condemnation, *he proclaims himself the Son of God*, they will see him *seated at the right of the Father coming on the clouds in Glory* (Mt. 26:63ff; Mk. 14:61ff; Lk. 22:69ff). And in the oldest of the Gospels Mark recounts his prayer at the opening of the Passion.

> and he said:
> Abba—Father,
> all things are possible for You.
> Take this cup from me,
> yet not what I desire
> but what You do.   (Mk. 14:36)

Mark preserves the Aramaic *Abba* in his Greek text as witness to the inner awareness of Christ: Jesus does not pray *Ab*, "*pater*", "*Father*"—in his agony he prays *Abba*, "*Daddy*".

3   Christ's own living consciousness of his identity within God is not centered upon abstractions, upon ideas of the relationship of God–and– Man. He *lives* the unfolding experience of personal existence. This is expressed *Abba*. It is not that God is actually a "parent" (or a "king" or "lord" or any *thing* else!); rather, Jesus recognizes himself responding to the Reality of God in the most intimate and unitive of personal relationships. "God is my Abba" expresses *person*, the Jesus who actually experiences as a person. He looks through the most intense human experience of personal origin—the generation of new living persons from parents—and affirms: Abba! And the sensitivity of that experience is expressed by *Abba* rather than *Father*: the childlike intensity of love and delight which knows only the uninhibited intimacy of Union.

Although the human word can be no more than a faith image of the inner experience of Christ, it opens the vision of that experience for us. We can *begin to see* if we know the experiential meaning of parent–and–child: begetting, bearing, nurturing, responding, loving.

Jesus not only proclaims *God is my Abba*, he prays *Abba!* And so he prays as no one else can. He does not *approach* God, *stand before* God, and *pray to* God. He prays as he himself actually exists, *within God*. Thus it is here that the ultimate questions of Faith and Prayer become one: *is he?* The life–long Tradition of the first disciples cannot imagine the possibility, for it is the Tradition of the gulf of separation between God and all of creation. Nothing comes forth from within God as God. No one can make himself Son to God. The faithful must pray to God in awe.

4   But Jesus prays *Abba!* And the disciples begin to grow in their own consciousness of Faith, and so they ask him to teach them to pray as he does. And we are taught, "say *Abba!*" As Christ teaches us how to begin to pray he calls for a total revolution in our consciousness *to be able to pray from within God*, no longer with any sense of distance. God as Transcendence —the Wholly Other—is a *fact*, but no longer of anything other than intellectual interest in a consciousness rightly dominated by the experience of being transformed in Union with Christ so that we actually begin to realize *we are within God*.

> For you have died
> and your life has been hidden with Christ in God;
> whenever Christ appears
> —he is our Life—
> you shall appear with him in Glory.   (Col. 3:3-4)

As we realize the wholeness of our unification within Christ, recognizing within him his integral Union in God, we realize there is no separation, no gulf of Transcendence: Transcendence is entered.

Traditions have called us to draw near to God, to experience His Compassion, to rejoice in His Presence—but we are to be in awe before the Absolute.

And Traditions have called us to lose ourselves in God, to experience absorption, to extinguish the falsity of self—but we cease in the Absolute.

Father and Son are truly One, yet Father is not Son. Jesus and each one of us are truly One and so we are truly One within Father and Son, yet no one of us is the other. Each one actually lives the Christ Life we wholly share. And so we truly pray *Abba!—our own Abba!*

5   *. . .say: Abba!*
     May Your Name be proclaimed Holy. . .

In the twenty centuries Christians have sought to pray as Jesus taught his first disciples, we have not been able to realize how they heard this acclamation. They listened to him from within the Tradition of Israel which gives profound meaning to *proclaiming the Holiness of the Divine Name.* Although we share so much with Israel in the person of Jesus and the testimony of the Scriptures, yet Gentile Christians have virtually no experience of the Hebrew Tradition. And so we think of this second statement of his prayer teaching as nothing more than an exclamation of piety. In reality it completes the recognition *God is Abba* by affirming our lives within God.

More than six hundred times the Torah of Moses records commands or prohibitions. For Israel living under the Covenant these have formed the pattern for life. As the heavens and earth have been given a Torah— the forces and laws of nature—so the human race has received a Torah. The Torah of nature is a determined and inexorable pattern: the stars in their course, the seasons, the tides, the times. The Torah given for people is also a pattern, but one of free response: to live obedient to its precepts leads to the natural perfection and happiness of human life. Though all peoples know at least some of the moral precepts through the light of conscience, it is to Israel that the full Torah was made known.

As the many precepts were given at different historic moments and never as abstractions but as concrete calls to the response of willing obedience, the pattern of the Torah must be interpreted in every generation to adapt it to ever-changing conditions of living communities. Essential to such interpretation is the determination of the differing degrees of importance of the various precepts relative to each other. (And hence the question: "Which is the first of all the commandments?" Mk. 12:23ff.)

6   With the shock of the Babylonian destruction of Israel, Jerusalem and the Temple, and then that of the Hellenistic persecution under Antiochus Epiphanes at the time of the Maccabees, the Teachers of the Torah realized that the text of the Torah could be destroyed by a determined tyrant and

even every Teacher who had learned the text could be killed. The gift of
the Torah, the perfect plan for human life, could be lost. But, they rea-
soned, God's gifts are not given in vain; there must be something within
the Torah itself whereby the gift can always be saved. And this they found
in one precept:

> You must not profane My Holy Name
> so that I may be proclaimed Holy
> among the sons of Israel,
> I YHWH Who make you holy.   (Lev. 22:32)

*To proclaim Holy the Name—Kiddush Ha-Shem—*is the work of those
whom God makes holy. This is the all–important center of Hebrew spirituality. But what does it mean to say *God is Holy?* This is to ask for the
inner understanding of the Mystery of God, the Mystery celebrated in the
hiddenness of the Name *I Am What I Am.* As the "Name" of God is His
own inner Self, so to proclaim Him "Holy" is to proclaim the inherent
Mystery the Transcendent always remains. *Kiddush,* the very word expressing
this proclamation of Holiness, reflects this hiddenness–experience, since
the Hebrew sense of the Holy indicates *set apart, cut off* from everything
else, the "profane". The fulfillment of this precept *Kiddush Ha-Shem* is not
a matter of *knowing* but of *living.* Humans created in the image of God
somehow can reflect at least a likeness of God's Holiness. God is proclaimed
Holy by people living lives of human holiness. The Hidden God can be
known reflectively in our own experience if our way of life follows the pattern set down in the Torah—as we live the pattern we can begin to realize
something of what it means to say *God is Holy.*

If the Torah were lost it could be recovered by remembering and fulfill-
ing the single precept *Kiddush Ha-Shem.* Each time a choice in life had
to be made one question would be asked: will this or will this not proclaim
the Holiness of God in human life? If we always chose that which did
manifest Divine Holiness, a lifetime of such choices would recreate the
pattern of perfection embodied in the Torah and so a lost Torah could be
recovered. It would not be in the historic form or words of the Mosaic Torah.
But the new form and words would contain the substance. To "walk in the
Law of the Lord" is to live in ultimate realism as a human being. This deep-
most meaning of *Kiddush Ha-Shem* is celebrated throughout the Psalms,
the Wisdom books, and all the prophetic understanding of covenantal
history.

7   In Christ there is a New Covenant—*a New Covenant in my Blood* (Lk. 22:30)—no longer an external relationship of a people dedicated to God in the observance of the Torah and God committed to them in promise. Christ himself is the Covenant, the *internal* relationship of unitive identity: All God is and all this man is are completely One, a Oneness including all of us in his Union. This New Covenant he—we are calls for something other than a Law, since any law must be a structure of relationships reaching out among individuals. The manifestation of the inner identity of Union must itself be the living Union—Love—

> This is His commandment:
> that we should believe in the Name of His Son Jesus Christ
> and love one another
> as he gave us commandment.
> Whoever keeps His commandments
> dwells in Him
> and He dwells in him.
> And by this we know He dwells in us
> by the Spirit He has given us.   (I Jn. 3:23-24)

To believe in his Name is to recognize and embrace the Given Son. To love one another is to recognize and embrace all to whom the Son is Given. We are to be so completely One that the world will realize the Father truly sent His Son and we are all loved with the same indivisible Love (Jn. 17:23).

We know the living unity, experiencing God from within, by the Gift of His own Spirit—His own living Self we now share. We fulfill the new *Kiddush Ha-Shem* in our new Christ Life, Giving the One we have been Given.

The entirety of Christ's instruction of what lies at the heart of our consciousness as we pray is contained in this two–fold opening of prayer: Father! May Your Name be proclaimed Holy—*Abba! Kiddush Ha-Shem*. We recognize: our identity is *within* God, we live His Life and share His Holiness. Jesus proclaims himself the living Covenant, not external to us, but reconstituting us in internal Union in God. And so for Christians there is Spirit, not Torah, as the generative moment of the prayerful experience of Faith actually lived—

No one has ever seen God.
If we love one another
God dwells in us
and His Love is perfected in us.
By this we know
we dwell in Him
and He in us:
because He has given us His Spirit.   (I Jn. 4:12–13)

8   *may Your Kingdom come...*

If we live the Christ Life the Kingdom comes *from within.*

The Kingdom of God does not come with observable signs,
nor will they say: see, it is here or there.
For the Kingdom of God is within you.   (Lk. 17:20–21)

Israel expected a kingdom as a political reality, restoring the lost kingdom of David. The "kingdom", however, is a symbol of what does indeed come in Christ: a new world of people in which God rules. But we must learn to recognize how God rules.

All power has been given to the Son who as Head of the Gathering—his living Body—is ruler of all. But he "rules" by giving himself so all can live. The God unveiled in Christ is not in the image of a human ruler: dominating, possessing, controlling. *God gives*—unconditionally, irreversibly, demanding nothing. *God gives in Love* so that we may live His Life.

God Given in Christ within human life is Head of the Gathering, that is, the Center of the person–with–person Gathering of all who together are the ever–extending reality of Incarnation.

There are no external signs of the Kingdom, none of the worldly evidences of human power, because the Kingdom is not of the old world. It is *God-with-us*, a truly new world. It is the rule of the Spirit: Giving. It cannot be found in some *place*—"here" or "there"—for it is the Union of persons *within* the Given God. It is not a city or a temple. It is people alive together sharing the Self–gift of God.

9   To pray for the coming of the Kingdom is to pray for the transforma-

tion of ourselves. It is our responsive reflection from within to the proclaiming of the Good News: Change! for the Kingdom of Heaven is near at hand (Mt.4:17). To pray for the Kingdom is to pray for our own awakening so that we will recognize how it is that God rules–by–Gift. But even more, it is to pray that we ourselves can begin to give the All we have received. We have been born again through the Giving Who is the Spirit and so have entered the Kingdom; we must now grow to maturity by our own Giving in the Spirit. The Kingdom is within us—among us in the midst of our shared Life—and we seek to change: from those who would lord it over others to those who really serve as God–in–Christ serves.

We do not pray for a Kingdom to come that never does come. It is not prayer for an always distant future. Christ has already poured out Life for us, and as he promised:

> Amen! I say to you:
> I will drink no more of the fruit of the vine
> until the day when I drink it new
> in the Kingdom of God.   (Mk.14:25)

We drink the new Wine with him: believing in him—recognizing him—and so never thirsting again, but drawing Life from him as he draws Life from the Father (Jn. 6:35,57). We enter the Kingdom through the Gift of rebirth, and pray that the Kingdom may come fully within us, as we grow in all ways into Christ by living the Truth and in Love (Eph. 4:15).

10   *give us each day our daily bread* . . .

> And do not seek
> what you might eat and drink
> and do not worry—
> the people of the world seek all these!
> Your Father knows you need them.
> But seek His Kingdom
> and these will be added as well.
> Fear not, little flock,
> Your Father is delighted
> to give you the Kingdom!   (Lk. 12:29–32)

Praying that the Kingdom may come fully within us calls us to the

awareness of our tangible lives. The Kingdom *within* is not a merely medi-
tative reality; it takes shape as we actually live. It is here, then, that we
pray in our need. But praying in need should not be imagined as *seeking
something*. Because the first moment of our prayer–consciousness is *Abba!*
we *know* our need is fulfilled completely in the One Who loves us absolutely. Our prayer might take the word–form of *asking* because of our tangible
need at this moment, but that is not the ultimate meaning in our depth
of Life where we recognize Abba.

Our daily bread is the bread for our daily lives, and it is *all* of the bread
we need to live the many moments of lives in transformation into Christ
Life. In this we confront a paradox:

> Do not work for food that does not last
> but for Food which endures to Eternal Life.   (Jn. 6:27)

Yet the Food of Christ Life is *Agape*, the Love that is self–giving, reaching
out to real people as they really are at this very moment. If they are materially
hungry then reaching out in Love must mean to reach out with hands
holding food for their bodily lives. If they hunger for someone to fill empty
lives then in Love we must offer our hands as friends. Whatever the hunger,
the call is for Love, but Love shaped for actual living persons.

> By this we have known Love
> because he laid down his life for us,
> and we ought to lay down our lives for our brothers.
> Whoever has the world's means of life
> and sees that his brother has need,
> and shuts his heart from him
> how does the Love of God dwell in him?
> My children,
> let us not love in word or in talk
> but in work and in truth.   (I Jn. 3:16–18)

The Food of Eternal Life is all our daily bread. As we pray, we *know*
God gives, and we know we have that same power to give. Food that cannot last is *mere things*—things taken for themselves and taken away from
persons. But these same things change value in our power to give, becoming things–for–persons and so becoming more of that Bread of Life we are
in the living Union we are in Christ.

In the root of our prayer–consciousness, *Abba! Kiddush Ha–Shem*, we discover we are not praying for God to give us something. We voice our trust in the Love which is already ours as pure Gift. And we will proclaim Holy the One Who gives *as we ourselves give*.

> . . . indeed, the Bread which I will give
> is my Flesh for the Life of the world.   (Jn. 6:51)

This is his promise already fulfilled, and so these become our words of promise in him to still others. As they asked him, so they ask us

> Lord, always give us this Bread!   (Jn. 6:34)

11   *and forgive us our sins*
   for we ourselves forgive everyone in debt to us . . .

We often find we are not seeking the Kingdom, but some thing instead. And how often we find ourselves shutting our hearts to others as we fasten on a thing.

> . . . the good I wish to do, I do not do,
> but I do the evil I really do not wish to do!   (Rm. 7:19)

We fail all too often, and even when we do not fail we feel the tension: life in transformation into Life.

We pray in our need to be *whole, undivided,* centered within the Christ Life from whose depths we cry out in delight *Abba!* It is the prayer–consciousness of regeneration—alien and stranger no longer, but truly sons and daughters *at–One*. We trust in the forgiveness of God. Our very word "forgive" suggests that trust: *give before*—before we need or ask we have been given the Love Who makes us One, Whole.

> In this has Love been perfected with us
> that we may have confidence
> in the day of judgment,
> because as He is
> so also are we in this world.

> There is no fear in love,
> but perfect Love casts out fear,
> because fear has torment
> and he who fears
> has not been perfected in Love.
> We love because He first loved us.   (I Jn. 4:17–19)

If we know absolutely that someone truly loves us, then we know we never have to fear that one. Fear arises because we cannot trust another—ultimately cannot trust him with our lives, since all our fears are rooted in the final fear of being destroyed. Someone who truly loves us will never wish to harm us willingly. We can trust one who loves us with our lives. Our willingness to live vulnerable-to-another is the tangible trust of love.

Perfect love casts out fear. . . It is not that we love God perfectly: *He is perfect Love.* The child trusts the love of the parent and so does not fear; it is not the love of the child for the parent that casts out fear, for the child must learn love through the experience of being loved first.

Jesus taught a new doctrine of forgiveness which, as with the unveiling of God as our Abba, both shocked and delighted his first hearers. The ancient doctrine of forgiveness was founded upon the process of justice. If one offended another a relationship of justice was destroyed and could only be restored by the forgiveness of the offense. But, of course, the one offended *did not have to forgive.* The offender had violated justice, and the bond with the other had been broken by his act. The one offended was not bound in justice to forgive the offense. The Tradition of Israel holds that even God cannot forgive an offense against another: the All-Just Lord cannot deprive the injured of their right to refuse to forgive which is the right to demand the exercise of justice.

This is the scandal of Jesus' forgiveness of Zacchaeus the Publican. As a tax-gatherer Zacchaeus had extorted money from the poor, deprived the defenseless of their means of life and, undoubtedly, had been the cause of final despair for many. His sins against justice were offenses against all of these people—so many he could not even begin to know all of them to seek their forgiveness, not to mention those who had died and so were unable to forgive. The orthodox taught that publicans put themselves beyond forgiveness since they dedicated their lives to sins crying out to Heaven for vengeance.

But Jesus forgives in *Agape*, not in justice. And he teaches: we must forgive as God forgives. To be in Christ Life we forgive freely those who think they are our enemies—*they do not know what they are doing*—and we forgive limitlessly:

> Peter came to him and asked:
> How often am I to forgive my brother
> who sins against me?
> Up to seven times?
> Jesus answered him:
> I tell you not up to seven times,
> but to seventy times seven!   (Mt. 18:21–22)

Seventy times "seven", the traditional symbol of limitless completion! We pray in trust as we feel our need for wholeness—either as restoration from failure, or as strengthening in the tension of good–and–evil we experience—recognizing the God Who so loves the world that He gives His Only Son that we might live and live fully. And as we realize forgiveness we recognize ourselves in that One Son forgiving all who have offended us.

If, indeed, we are as surprised as his first hearers by the freedom of his forgiveness—forgiving others *in spite of* our not forgiving them—then our prayer for forgiveness begins to take on a new meaning for us. We begin to realize: we have the power to forgive. We begin to desire reconciliation with one another. We can *forgive from the heart*, that is, from the ultimate Center of ourselves. We forgive as God forgives, *first* and in *Agape*: as we have been loved so we begin to know how to love. Because we love, no one has to fear us!

12   *and do not bring us to the test.*

The calling of ancient Israel to Faith is the call to the recognition of God as the One Alone to be loved:

> Hear, O Israel, the Lord our God, the Lord is One
> and you shall love the Lord your God
> with all your heart
> and with all your self
> and with all your might.   (Deut. 6:4–5)

And the response of Faith is to the awesome God Who must never be doubted:

You shall not put the Lord your God to the test . . .   (Deut. 6:16)

But over and over again in Israel's history God is doubted and the people insist on "proof" of God's power, putting Him to the test. And each time they are punished for their faithlessness, for not loving with whole heart, self and might.

Yet, throughout the Hebrew Scriptures, God is portrayed as testing people, from the first opening of creation to the final expectation of the Messiah. Abraham is tested to see if he is worthy: will he kill his only son to prove himself to God? The Israelites are drawn into the desert wastes to see if they are worthy: will they trust the Lord in His promise of a land flowing with milk and honey? The people are enslaved in the Babylonian exile to see if they are worthy: will they repent and prepare themselves humbly for a Liberator?

When we truly love another *we do not test*, requiring proof of love in return as the condition of our love. True love in depth proclaims trust— and hence the sense of vulnerability in loving: being open to the other, trusting the response will be love. We are not to *test* God because, loving Him wholly we trust Him wholly. And teaching us to pray, Jesus teaches us to realize *we are not put to any test*. If we can pray *Abba* then we know God absolutely loves us, and there is no testing in love. To seek "proof" of love destroys it. The child who experiences love from a parent will have to doubt that love if the parent demands "proof" of the child's responding love.

Agape is love–by–giving, and if it is truly *giving* then there can be no conditions. To demand "love me, then I will love you" is not to *give* but to *purchase*. God loves/gives absolutely: we are loved even before we exist— we exist because we are loved.

And we are taught in prayer *to trust*: we will not be put to any test, because we know we are loved first and our response of love is true. The One we recognize with joy as our *Abba* does not probe us to see if we are worthy of Him, He demands no supposed proofs, He sets no conditions. He loves even if we do not love in return. His Self–gift is ours irrevocably even if we refuse to receive.

13   We pray *Abba!* and everything else in prayer flows from that one realization—*we are loved*.

Kiddush Ha-Shem: we consecrate ourselves to lives that embrace that Love and so become loving lives for others.

The Kingdom: we seek our transformation from within so that the real rule of God can be recognized: God Given and Giving.

Our bread: our tangible needs and those of all who share life with us, drawn into consciousness of trust as we set our hearts first and always on the Kingdom.

Forgiveness: we are free in the Love God is as the unique Gift of Life, in Whom we are made whole and have the power to heal others.

Beyond test: we can trust the Love God is, Who demands nothing, but simply *gives*.

The first disciple realized Jesus prayed like no other before him. And he taught them—us to pray his way: say *Abba!*

PRAYER AS ONE SPIRIT: TRUTH

1   In the Tradition of Israel the first disciples expected Jesus to pray *to* God. However present God might be, God and a human being remained ultimately *not in interior union*. We cannot begin to appreciate the shock that took place as they realized: He prays *with* God, he prays *from within* and not outwards towards "another". That the shock was positive we know from the fact that they wanted to learn to pray as he prayed. This can all seem obvious until we remind ourselves that, typically, we do not pray *with/within* God but *to* God.

We are always reaching out to "contact" God Who is, therefore, not seen by us as *within*. In prayer we find ourselves speaking to Someone Else, rather than being conscious of ourselves *in interior Union with* the One *within* Whom we live. The disciples asked Jesus to teach them to pray the new way they observed in him, and he did. Our problem in prayer is simple: we do not pray *that way*. We have changed our expectation, so that when we pray we expect to be addressing Someone Else—however loving and close—nevertheless *distanced* as an object to which we attempt to relate as subjects.

In the Matthean parallel to the Lucan presentation of Jesus' prayer teaching we find that teaching transformed into an actual form of prayer, most probably used antiphonally in the earliest Liturgy. That form reinforces the expectation of praying *within* God in the opening affirmation,

Our Abba . . . If they really meant *Our* Abba this had to be blasphemy; the violent reaction of persecution in those first years of the Gathering in Palestine tells us clearly what the disciples communicated by their words. Jesus had been condemned because he had made God his Abba, and the disciples were also condemned for insisting God indeed is his Abba and their own also.

2   Apart from using the word Abba alone, only the modifiers "my" or "our" can be used without any danger of changing the essential expectation of this way of praying. The Abba "in Heaven" or the "Heavenly Abba" had become the common symbol for the Godhead rather than the archaic notion of the "place" where God dwelt upon the throne of Glory. Yet, in time, the symbolism of a Heaven–place asserted itself and the Abba "in Heaven" expressed distance. With the possible exceptions of "Loving Father" or "Living Father" virtually any word or image creates a sense of distance. "Almighty Father" or even "Our Almighty Father" insists on a consciousness of separation (He may well be Father to me/us in some way, but He is Might–Power–Creator, while I simply am not!). We can observe this change in consciousness in the evolution of the liturgical prayer forms. Paul speaks of the Christ we experience as embodying in himself all of our fulfillment and so it is within him that we pray—

> In him is the *Yes!*
> to the many promises of God.
> Therefore it is *through him*
> that we respond *Amen!*
> to the Glory of God.   (II Cor. 1:20)

Paul's expectation is to pray *within* Christ who contains All in Union: God Given to us, we drawn into Him. Although the address *to* God *through* Christ can imply distance in the very structure of the words, yet it is possible to "move across" this distance by remembering we are one in Union in Christ, and so prayer *through* him can "take us with him". This is certainly a prayer expectation commonly expressed in many apostolic writings. But the further development in liturgical forms draws resolutely away from this sensitivity, and distance is firmly reestablished. God is prayed *to*, the Trinitarian formulas put Christ as Son psychologically on the "other side"; the saints of the community sharing the unity of life also gradually shift

to that "other side" and become intercessors between God and the one
who prays. The various response forms for the liturgical prayers and related
litanies reinforce this distance dramatically, as a series of petition prayers
is answered over and over with "Lord have mercy" or "Lord hear our prayer"
and the like. The same psychological pattern affects all: We "here below"
pray to and through others "above in Heaven", ultimately to God Father–
Son–Spirit, Who has become *in expectation* as separated from us as the image
of the Lord God of the Torah. The revolution in our prayer–consciousness
is thus theologically "postponed"—in the eschatological future, when *after
death* we dwell in God and He dwells in us, then as we see Him as He really
is. . . And we have forgotten that moment in the Last Supper

> the hour is coming
> when I will make the Father known to you plainly.
> On that day you will ask in my Name,
> and I do not say *I shall ask the Father for you*
> for the Father Himself loves you. . .   (Jn. 16:25–27)

We are to pray *in the Name* of Jesus—within his self–reality now given to
us, the identity we now share; he will not ask for us. He is the unifying
Mediator, not a mediator who stands between us and God merely bridg-
ing the separation. Within Christ there is no separation. And it is within
him that we have our Life. This should be our prayer–consciousness.

3   There are many factors at the root of the early drift away from the prayer
from–within–God to prayer outwards–towards God. In terms of Traditions,
all the prayer of Israel is necessarily outwards–towards and so the use of
the Scriptural prayers, especially the Psalter, continually reasserts the not–
from–within expectation. All the attempts to "reinterpret" psalms Christo-
logically notwithstanding, the very *form* of the words teaches people to
pray outwards–towards and not the way Jesus taught, from–within. The
psalms simply do not and cannot have this expectation. And so in their
tangible form they must run counter to and ultimately undermine the new
Christ prayer–consciousness.

The Matthean "Lord's Prayer" form introduced other problems, in the
ambiguous meaning of "Heaven" and in the dialogue–effect achieved in
the antiphonal shape. As we realize, "Heaven" can be an image of separation if it is used in a cosmological theology, especially as this affects the
folk–level of religion. But again, in the radical change of expectation ex-

perienced in Christ, the disciples were taught a new meaning for "heaven". Not only was it no longer a cosmological place, it was no longer a designation for Divinity at a distance of Transcendence. There is an intensely personal–communal meaning: Heaven is within, in each and in the midst of all gathered together as One. God–in–Christ is the Center of our Union of lives as Life. In that meaning "Our Father in Heaven. . ." can dramatically reinforce the sense of prayer from–within the now inherent unity in consciousness of people–with–God. The coming of the Kingdom is then no mere aspiration for some day in the time–distanced future, but another deepening of the sense of from–within, since the revolution in expectation extends to the Messianic Kingdom which is not to be an external rule by God from on high, but is to come from–within and be within the new form of Life begun in Christ–Union.

The great problem of prayer from–within rests with us as we are, regardless of the expectations molded by our heritages. The plain fact is that the development of a life of prayer from–within–God is extraordinarily demanding. It embodies the most basic *conversion*, a constitutional change, or in the fundamental term of spirituality, a true *metanoia*. It is clearly easier to see oneself as a mere creature dutifully *approaching* God—Who therefore remains safely "outside". We can thus avoid the self–responsibility inevitable in truly participating in the Fullness of All God is. Untransformed, we really prefer to postpone this wonderful destiny for some later phase of our existence. It is easier and surer to take only the responsibility of a *creature responding to* God, and not to enter into our co–creativity with God.

Once again, this is exemplified in the parallel passages of Luke and Matthew on the significance of prayer. Prayer is always "answered", as Matthew (7:11) gives Christ's teaching:

> If therefore you who can do evil
> know how to give good gifts to your children,
> how much more will your Father in Heaven
> give good things to those who ask Him?   (Mt. 7:11)

But Luke (11:13) understands Christ's teaching with a very different expectation:

> . . . how much more will your Father in Heaven
> give the Holy Spirit to those who ask Him?   (Lk. 11:13)

We are not promised "good things", but the very Power of God, the Spirit Who transforms us into the new Christ Life in which we are member-for-member Christ Living in his bodily Resurrection.

Unquestionably this promised answer to prayer profoundly inspires and attracts. But on second thought we really would prefer to have "good things" rather than the Power within us to create for ourselves. It is easier to be faithful/obedient by waiting to receive *from* God outside us. It requires a less developed sense of responsibility. God "out there" need not be the primitive sense and image of a multi-storeyed world with a Heaven-place at a distance from our world and daily life. The "out there" can be an infinitesimal distance—God present, yes, but safely not from-within.

Prayer from within the Reality of God is the prayer of Truth, for our truest utterance is *Abba!* This we cry out in the Power of the Spirit now ours, the Power of the inmost Depth of God which we begin to realize is the source and answer to all our prayer.

> The hour is coming—it is now!—
> when true worshippers
> will worship the Father
> in Spirit and Truth—
> for, indeed, the Father seeks such to worship Him.
> God is Spirit
> and those who worship
> must worship in Spirit and Truth.   (Jn. 4:23–24)

six

FURTHER SCRIPTURAL WITNESSES

THE GOOD NEWS: CHRIST

1   Romans 1

    3   . . . His Son
        descended of the seed of David
        according to the flesh,
    4   proclaimed in Power
        Son of God
        according to the Spirit of Holiness
        through his resurrection from among the dead:
        Jesus Christ our Lord!

2   I Timothy 3

    16   Undeniably great is the mystery of religion:
        He was manifested in the flesh,
        affirmed in the Spirit,

seen by the messengers,
proclaimed among the peoples,
believed by the world,
exalted in Glory!

ONENESS IN CHRIST

1   Galatians 2

19   For through the Law
     I died to the Law
     that I might live to God.
     I have been crucified–together–with Christ,
20   and I live no more,
     but Christ lives in me;
     and what I now live in the flesh
     I live by Faith in the Son of God
     who loved me
     and gave himself up for me.

2   Galatians 3

26   For you all are Sons of God
     through Faith in Christ Jesus.
27   For as many of you as have been baptized into Christ,
     you have put on Christ.
28   There is neither Jew nor Greek,
     neither slave nor freeman,
     neither male nor female,
     for you are all One in Christ Jesus.

PARTICIPATION IN CHRIST

Romans 6

1   What, then, do we say—

should we continue in sin
so that Gift might increase?

2 Never!
We have died to sin
so how can we still live in it?

3 Or are you unaware
that as we were all baptized into Christ Jesus
we were baptized into his death?

4 For through baptism
we were buried–together–with him in his death
so that as Christ was raised from among the dead
through the Glory of the Father
so we also might walk
in newness of Life.

5 For if we have become One with him
in the sameness of his death,
we shall also be One
in his resurrection.

6 We thus realize:
our former self was crucified–together–with him
that the body of sin might be destroyed
so that we should no longer serve sin,

7 for anyone who has died
has been set free from sin.

8 But if we died with Christ
we believe we also shall live–together–with him,

9 realizing that Christ having been raised
from among the dead
never again dies,
never again does death have power over him.

10 For as he died
he died to sin
once for all time,
but as he lives
he is alive for God.

11 And therefore you must be aware of yourselves
as truly dead to sin
but alive for God
in Christ Jesus.

THE MYSTERY OF FAITH

1   Colossians 1

9   . . .
     we have not ceased praying for you
     and asking that you may be filled
     with the whole knowledge of His Will
     in all wisdom and spiritual understanding,

10   to walk worthily of the Lord,
     pleasing in everything,
     bearing fruit in every good work
     and growing in the whole knowledge of God,

11   endowed with all Power
     by the might of His own Glory,
     to have real endurance and patience,

12   giving thanks with joy to the Father
     Who made you fit to share
     the lot of the saints in Light.

13   He has delivered us from the dominion of darkness
     and transferred us to the realm
     of the Son of His Love.

14   In him we have redemption,
     the forgiveness of our sins.
     . . .

21   Once you were estranged
     and enemies in your mind
     by your evil works,

22   but now he has reconciled you
     in the body of his flesh through his death,
     to present you
     holy and faultless and irreproachable
     before Him,

23   if you continue in the Faith
     grounded and steadfast and unmoveable
     from the hope of the Good News you have heard,
     which has been proclaimed
     throughout all creation under heaven,

of which I, Paul, have become a minister

. . .

2   Colossians 2

1   I wish you to know
     how great a struggle I have for you
     and those in Laodicea
     and for the many others
     who have not seen my face in the flesh—
2   so that their hearts may be comforted
     being joined together in Love,
     for all the wealth
     of the full assurance of understanding,
     for full knowledge
     of the Mystery of God
     —Christ—
3   in whom are hidden all the treasures
     of wisdom and knowledge.
4   I say this so no one may deceive you
     with specious arguments.
5   For if, indeed, I am absent in the flesh
     yet I am with you in the spirit
     rejoicing to see your harmony
     and the firmness of your Faith in Christ.
6   As you have received Christ Jesus the Lord
     walk in him!—
7   having been rooted and built up in him
     and being held firm
     in the Faith you were taught,
     overflowing in thanksgiving.
8   Be on your guard against anyone robbing you
     through mere philosophy,
     some empty deceit
     derived from human tradition
     according to the principles of the world
     and not according to Christ—
9   For in him dwells

all the Fullness of the Godhead bodily.
10   And you yourselves have been filled completely in him
who is the head of all rule and authority,
11   and in whom you were circumcised
not with a handwrought circumcision,
but by putting off the body of the flesh
in the circumcision of Christ
12   buried–together–with him in baptism,
you were also raised–together–with him
through Faith in the Power of God
raising him from the dead.
13   You were dead in your sins
and in the uncircumcision of your flesh,
but he brought you to life–together–with him
forgiving you all your sins,
14   wiping out what was written against us
in the Precepts
he has taken it from our midst
and nailed it to the Cross;
15   overthrowing the rulers and authorities
he paraded them as prisoners in public
triumphing over them in it.
16   Therefore, let no one call you to account
concerning eating or drinking
or a feast or new–moon or sabbaths—
17   such is but a shadow of what is coming:
the Body of Christ!
18   Let no one ensnare you
desiring you to grovel in spirit–worship
by claiming visions,
19   vainly puffed up by his mind of flesh,
not in Union with the Head
from whom the whole Body,
strengthened and held together
through its joints and sinews,
will grow with the growth given by God.
20   If you truly died with Christ
to the principles of the world,

why do you let yourselves be bound to its rules
as if you lived in the world?

. . .

3   Colossians 3

9   . . .you have stripped off
     the old self with his practices
10 and have put on the new one
     in full awareness of the Image
     of the One Who creates him.
11 Here divisions have no place—
     Greek and Jew,
     circumcision and uncircumcision,
     barbarian, Scythian,
     slave, freeman—
     but Christ is All and in all!
12 Therefore, as those chosen by God
     who are holy and loved,
     be clothed with inmost–felt compassion,
     with kindness, humility, meekness, long–suffering,
13 being patient with one another
     and generously forgiving each other
     when anyone has a complaint against another.
     As the Lord has forgiven you
     so you must do.
14 And over all these garments
     bind them together with Love
     which is the bond of perfection.
15 And let the Peace of Christ
     rule in your hearts,
     for to this you were called together
     into one Body.
     Be thankful!
16 Let the Word of Christ
     indwell richly within you,
     as in all Wisdom
     you teach and advise each other.

And in psalms, hymns and spiritual songs
sing with gratitude in your hearts to God.

17   And whatever you do
in Word or in Work
do all in the Name of the Lord Jesus
giving thanks to God the Father
through him.

CHRIST THE UNIFYING PEACE

Ephesians 2

13   . . . in Christ Jesus
you who once were far away
have been brought near
by the Blood of Christ.

14   For he is our Peace:
he made the two into one,
breaking down the wall
which kept us apart,
in his own flesh
destroying the hostility

15   which arose through the decrees
of the Law of Commandments,
so that he could create
One New Human Being
within himself,
and thus make Peace,

16   and reconcile both to God
in One Body
through the Cross,
putting hostility to death
in his own person.

17   And then he came
preaching Peace to those far off
and Peace to those near at hand,

18   for through him

we both have access
to the Father
in the One Spirit.

UNIVERSAL REBIRTH IN SPIRIT

Romans 8

18   I consider that the present sufferings
are not worthy to be compared
with the coming Glory
to be unveiled to us.
19   For the anxious expectation of all creation
eagerly awaits the revelation
of the offspring of God.
20   For creation was subjected to futility
not purposefully of its own intent
but through the one Who put it into subjection
—yet with hope,
21   because even creation itself will be liberated
from the slavery of corruption
into the freedom
of the Glory of the offspring of God.
22   For we know all creation until now
groans–together and suffers–together–in–birth–pains.
23   Not only creation but also ourselves,
we who have the first–fruits of the Spirit,
we also groan within ourselves
eagerly awaiting adoption,
the freeing of our bodies.
24   For we are saved foreseeing through hope;
but hope seen realized is not hope—
why should one merely hope
if he actually sees it realized?
25   But if what we hope for
we do not yet see realized,
then with patience we eagerly expect it.

26   And the Spirit also comes–together–with us
     to help in our weakness,
     for what prayer we should make
     we do not know,
     but the Spirit Herself intercedes for us
     with birth–groanings beyond expression.
27   And He Who examines hearts
     knows the Mind of the Spirit—
     because it is according to the Mind of God
     that She makes supplication
     on behalf of the saints.
28   And we know that for those who love God
     He works–together–with them
     turning all things to their good,
     those who are called according to His purpose.
29   Because those He foreknew He foreordained
     that they be formed–together–into
     the image of His Son,
     that he should be the first–born of many brothers.
30   Those He foreordained, He called,
     and those He called, He made just,
     and those He made just, He glorified!

LIVING SPIRIT

II Corinthians 3

2   You are our letter
    written in our hearts
    known and read by all.
3   It is clear you are a Letter of Christ
    delivered by us—
    not written in ink
    but in the Spirit of the Living God.
    not on stone tablets
    but on tablets of living hearts.
4   We have this confidence in God through Christ—

5 not that we are capable of claiming
anything comes from ourselves
but our capacity comes from God
6 who made us competent ministers
of a New Covenant
not written in letters
but in Spirit—
for the letter kills
but Spirit gives Life.

CHRIST UNION

1   I Corinthians 3

21 So let no one boast about men—
for all things are yours,
22 whether Paul or Apollos or Cephas,
or the world,
or life or death,
or the present or the future—
all things are yours
and you are Christ's
and Christ is God's!

2   Ephesians 2

19 Therefore, no longer are you foreigners and visitors.
but you are fellow citizens of the saints
and members of the family of God.
20 You have been built on the foundation
of the apostles and prophets
and Christ Jesus himself is the cornerstone,
21 in whom the entire building is fitted together
and grows into a holy Temple in the Lord,
22 and in whom you are being built together
into a dwelling–place of God
in the Spirit.

3   I Peter 2

1   Therefore put away all malice and all guile
     and hypocrisy and envy and all detraction.
2   As newborn infants
     desire the pure–consciousness milk,
     so that you may grow up to salvation
3   as you have tasted that the Lord is good.
4   Set yourselves close to him
     for he is a living stone
     rejected by people
     but chosen by God—costly!
5   And you yourselves as living stones
     are being built into a spiritual House
     to be a holy priesthood
     to offer spiritual sacrifices
     made acceptable to God by Jesus Christ.
6   For it is written in Scripture:
     See! In Zion I lay a chosen stone,
     the costly cornerstone,
     and no one who believes in him
     will be disappointed.
7   To you who believe, he is precious,
     but for the unbelievers
     the stone the builders rejected
     has become the cornerstone.
8   And it is a stumbling stone
     and an injuring rock,
     and those who disobey
     stumble over the Word
9   as, indeed, they were destined.
     But you are a chosen race,
     a royal priesthood,
     a holy nation,
     a people set apart,
     so that you might sing forth praises of Him
     Who called you out of darkness
     into His wondrous Light.

10 Once you were not a people
    but now you are a people of God.
    Once you had not received compassion
    but now you experience it.

4   Romans 12

    1 So I beseech you, brothers,
       by the Compassion of God,
       to present your bodies
       a living, holy sacrifice
       well pleasing to God,
       your conscious worship.
    2 And do not be aligned to this age
       but be transformed
       by renewing your mind
       so you may discern
       what is the will of God
       which is good, pleasing and perfect.

THE REALITY OF LOVE

I Corinthians 12

31 Eagerly desire the greater gifts
    and I shall show you a way
    far exceeding any other.

I Corinthians 13

    1 If I should speak with *gift of tongues*
       of people and of angels
       but not have Love—
       then I am only a gong booming
       or a cymbal clashing!
    2 And if I have *gift of prophecy*
       and grasp all mysteries and all knowledge,

and even if I have *fullness* of Faith
to be able to move mountains
but not have Love—
I am nothing!

3   And if I give away all my possessions
and even hand over my body to be burned
but not have Love—
it does me no good!

4   Love is patient,
Love is kind,
Love is not jealous,
it is not boastful, not conceited,
5   it is not rude, not selfish,
it does not take offense, is not resentful.
6   It takes no pleasure in another's sin
but rejoices in the Truth:
7   it excuses all, believes all,
trusts all, endures all.

8   Love never fails,
whereas *prophecies* will pass away,
and *tongues* will cease,
and even knowledge will pass.
9   For we know only in fragments
and we prophesy only in fragments,
10   but when that which is Whole comes
then that made of fragments passes away.
11   When I was a child
I spoke as a child
I thought as a child
I argued as a child.
Now that I have become an adult
I have put aside a child's ways!
12   Now we can only see a blur
as in a mirror reflection,
but then it will be face–to–face!
Now I only know a fragment
but then I shall fully know

just as I am fully known!

13   For the present there are these three:
     Faith, Hope, Love,
     and the greatest of these—Love!

BLESSING IN CHRIST

Ephesians 1

3   Blessed be the God and Father
     of our Lord Jesus Christ
     Who has blessed us
     with every spiritual blessing
     in the Heavens in Christ!
4   He chose us in him
     before the foundation of the world
     that we should be holy and unblemished,
     present to Him in Love,
5   He foreordained us to our adoption
     as His own offspring
     through Jesus Christ
     by His generous purpose,
6   to the praise of the Glory of His Gift
     with which He gifted us
     in the One He loved.
7   In him we gain our freedom
     through his Blood,
     the forgiveness of sins.
     Such is the richness of His Gift
8   which He gave superabundantly to us
     in all wisdom and knowledge,
9   making known to us
     the Mystery of His Will—
     according to His own purpose,
     He intended it to be hidden within Himself
10   to be the provision for the fullness of time:
     all things brought to their Head in Christ,

both those of Heaven and those of earth.

11   And in him we were claimed as His own,
chosen according to the purpose
of the One Who does all things
by the guidance of His own Will,

12   and this so we should be
the praise of His Glory,
we who already trusted in Christ.

13   In him you also trust,
now that you hear the message of Truth,
the Good News of your salvation,
and as you believe in him
you are sealed
with the Holy Spirit of the Promise.

14   He is the guarantee of our inheritance
in the freeing of those He possesses
as the praise of His Glory.

EUCHARISTIC CHRIST LIFE

John 6

35   I AM the Bread of Life.
The one who comes to me
shall never hunger
and the one who believes in me
shall never thirst.

36   But as I told you
you have seen me
yet you do not believe.

37   All the Father gives me
will come to me,
and whoever comes to me
I will never turn away.

38   For I have come down from Heaven
not to do my own will

but the Will of the One Who sent me.

39   And the Will of the One Who sent me is
that I should lose none
of all He has given me
but should raise it up
on the last day.

40   For this is the Will of my Father:
everyone who sees the Son
and believes in him
shall have Eternal Life
and I will raise him up
on the last day.

. . .

44   No one can come to me
unless the Father Who sent me draws him,
and I will raise him up
on the last day.

45   It has been written in the prophets:
And they shall all be taught by God.
Anyone who hears and learns from the Father
comes to me!

46   Not that anyone has seen the Father—
except the One Who IS with God,
he has seen the Father.

47   Amen! Amen! I say to you:
He who believes has Eternal Life—

48   I AM the Bread of Life.

49   Your fathers ate the manna in the desert
and died!

50   but this is the Bread coming down from Heaven
so that anyone may eat it
and not die!

51   I AM the living Bread
who has come down from Heaven.
If anyone eats this Bread
he will live forever.
And indeed the Bread I shall give
is my flesh,

for the Life of the world

. . .

53 Amen! Amen! I say to you:
Unless you eat the flesh of the Son of Man
and drink his blood
you shall not have Life in you.

54 He who eats my flesh
and drinks my blood
has Eternal Life,
and I will raise him up
on the last day.

55 For my flesh is true food
and my blood is true drink.

56 He who eats my flesh
and drinks my blood
dwells in me
and I in him.

57 As the Living Father sent me
and I live because of the Father
so he who eats me
will himself live because of me.

58 This is the Bread come down from Heaven—
not like that our ancestors ate,
they died!
he who eats this Bread
will live forever!

. . .

63 It is the Spirit Who gives Life,
the flesh achieves nothing.
The words I have spoken to you
are Spirit and are Life!

. . .

66 (Because of this teaching
many of his disciples turned back
and no longer walked with him.)

67 So Jesus said to the Twelve:
Do you also wish to go?

68 Simon Peter answered him:

Master, to whom shall we go?
You have the words of Eternal life!
And we believe and know:
You are the Holy One of God!

FAITH AND LOVE

I John 1

1   That which was from the beginning
which we have heard
which we have seen with our eyes
which we have beheld
and our hands have touched:
the Word of Life!—

2   And the Life was revealed
and we have seen
and we bear witness
and we announce to you
the Eternal Life
which was with the Father
and was revealed to us—

3   That which we have seen and heard
we announce to you
so that you may have unity with us.
And truly our unity is with the Father
and with His Son Jesus Christ.

4   And we write these things
that our joy may be fulfilled.

   . . .

I John 2

12   I write to you, little children,
because your sins have been forgiven you
for the sake of his Name.

13   I write to you, parents,

because you have known him
Who IS from the beginning.
I write to you, young people,
because you have overcome the evil one.

14 I have written to you, children,
because you have known the Father.
I have written to you, parents,
because you have known him
Who IS from the beginning.
I have written to you, young people,
because you are strong
and the Word of God dwells in you
and you have overcome the evil one.

. . .

24 That which you heard from the beginning
let it dwell in you.
If that which you heard from the beginning
dwells in you
you will dwell
both in the Son and in the Father.

25 And this is the promise that he promised us:
Eternal Life!

. . .

27 And the Anointing you have received from him
dwells in you
and you have no need
that anyone teach you.
But as his Anointing teaches you all things
and is true and is not a lie,
and as it has taught you
so dwell in him.

28 And now, little children, dwell in him
that when he is revealed
we may have confidence
and not be ashamed before him
at his appearing.

29 And if you know that he is just
know also that everyone who practices justice

has been born of him.

. . .

I John 4

  7   Beloved, let us love one another
        because Love is of God
        and everyone who loves
        has been begotten of God
        and knows God.
  8   He who does not love
        does not know God—
        for God is Love!
  9   By this the Love of God was revealed to us:
        because God has sent
        His Only–Begotten Son
        into the world
        that we might live through him.
10   In this is Love
        not that we have loved God
        but that He has loved us
        and has sent His Son
        as sacrifice for our sins!
11   Beloved, if God so loved us
        we ought to love one another.
12   No one has ever seen God
        but if we love one another
        God dwells in us
        and His Love is made perfect in us.
13   By this we know
        we dwell in Him
        and He in us
        because He has given us His Spirit.

14   And we have beheld and bear witness
        that the Father has sent the Son
        as Savior of the world.
15   Whoever witnesses that Jesus is the Son of God

God dwells in him
and he in God.
16   And we have known and have believed
the Love God has for us.
God is Love
and he who dwells in Love
dwells in God
and God dwells in him.

17   In this has Love been perfected with us
that we may have confidence
in the day of judgment,
because as He is
so also are we in this world.
18   There is no fear in Love
but perfect Love casts out fear,
because fear has torment
and he who fears has not been perfected in Love.
19   We love because He first loved us!

20   If anyone says *I love God*
and hates his brother,
he is a liar!
For he who does not love his brother
whom he has seen
cannot love God
Whom he has not seen.
21   And this commandment we have from Him:
he who loves God
loves his brother also.

MYSTERY IN GLORY

1   Romans 11

33   Oh, the depth of the riches
and wisdom and knowledge of God!
How unfathomable are His decisions

and how untrackable are His ways!

34   For who ever knew the Mind of the Lord,
or who ever became His advisor?

35   Or who ever loaned to Him
so as to deserve repayment himself?

36   For all things exist
from Him and through Him and for Him!
His is the Glory
for all ages, Amen!

2   Romans 16

25   To Him Who is able to ground you firmly
in my preaching of the Good News
and proclamation of Jesus Christ,
by the disclosure of the Mystery

26   kept hidden throughout endless ages
but, as witnessed by the prophetic writings,
now made manifest
and made known to all the peoples
through the command of the Eternal God
to bring them to the obedient response of Faith—

27   to God who alone is Wise,
give Glory age after age
through Jesus Christ.
Amen!

3   I Timothy 6

15   . . .the Appearing of our Lord Jesus Christ
which the joyous and only Ruler
will reveal in its own time:
the King of kings and Lord of lords,

16   who alone possesses immortality,
who dwells in inaccessible Light,
whom no one has seen or can see—
to him be honor and eternal might,
Amen!